D0589538

Communicating
with Learners
in the Lifelong Learning Sector

Communicating
with Learners
in the Lifelong Learning Sector

Nancy Appleyard and Keith Appleyard

LRC Stoke Park
GUILDFORD COLLEGE

LearningMatters

374.1102
APP
180424

Acknowledgements

We would like to thank the following for their help and support:

Susan Hobbes, Fraser White and staff at Stephenson College;
Sandie Stratford, Viv Channing, Lorna Page and the ITT trainees at Lincoln College;
Veronica Capaldi;
Amy Thornton and Clare Weaver.

First published in 2010 by Learning Matters Ltd

All rights reserved. No part of this publication may be reproduced, stored in a retrieval system, or transmitted in any form or by any means, electronic, mechanical, photocopying, recording, or otherwise, without prior permission in writing from Learning Matters.

© 2010 Nancy Appleyard and Keith Appleyard

British Library Cataloguing in Publication Data
A CIP record for this book is available from the British Library.

ISBN: 978 1 84445 377 1

The right of Nancy Appleyard and Keith Appleyard to be identified as the authors of this work has been asserted by them in accordance with the Copyright, Designs and Patents Act 1988.

Cover design by Topics – The Creative Partnership
Text design by Code 5
Project management by Deer Park Productions, Tavistock, Devon
Typeset by PDQ Typesetting Ltd, Newcastle under Lyme
Printed and bound in Great Britain by Cromwell Press Group, Trowbridge, Wiltshire

Learning Matters
33 Southernhay East
Exeter EX1 1NX
Tel: 01392 215560
info@learningmatters.co.uk
www.learningmatters.co.uk

Contents

About the authors

Nancy Appleyard has been teaching communication studies and personal development to a wide range of adults since 1994. Initially she worked as a tutor at Lincoln College teaching government funded programmes for returners to education. Since 2001 she has designed and developed more wide-ranging and flexible communication and personal development programmes within the FE sector and voluntary organisations.

Keith Appleyard has worked within the post-16 sector since 1978 as a lecturer, college senior manager and teacher trainer. He has been a tutor and course leader for PGCE/Cert Ed programmes at Lincoln College, and a tutor on these programmes at Nottingham Trent University. He is presently an ITT reviewer for Standards Verification UK (SVUK).

1
Introduction

I'm anxious about:
- *lasting out for two hours and keeping the class interested and motivated;*
- *getting the learners to like me;*
- *my poor spelling;*
- *being on show and giving a lecture;*
- *students asking questions that I don't know the answers to;*
- *dealing with students who know more than me and keep challenging me;*
- *students running riot.*

These quotations are a selection of responses we received from some Diploma in Teaching in the Lifelong Learning Sector (DTLLS) trainees who helped us in the research for this book, and they were reflecting on their feelings when they first started teaching. Did any of their responses strike a chord with you? They certainly did with us, as we look back at the various terrors we experienced when we first walked into a classroom. What we found striking about these responses is that all of them relate to how the trainees communicated with learners. It brings home the fact that good communication is a key teaching skill that can make the difference between a massively rewarding experience and a nightmare. This book is about developing your communication with your learners so that you don't have nightmares but lots of rewarding experiences in your professional role.

You may remember a film called *Dead Poets' Society*. It tells the story of John Keating, an English teacher who inspired his pupils through his teaching of poetry and literature. Keating inspired his pupils so powerfully because he was able to project his enthusiasm and stimulate a similar and equally powerful feeling in his students. And the way he did it was through communication, not merely using the skills of speaking and listening, but also through his ability to project his own feelings and to value and respect the people he was teaching. If you get the chance, try to see this film because it encapsulates what this book is about: the ability of teachers to change lives, expressed through their communication skills.

Communicating with learners is more than speaking clearly and writing good handouts. You are communicating on many levels from the very moment you meet your learners. Everything they see and hear, the way you have arranged the furniture, what you are wearing, in fact, the whole pattern of your behaviour, conveys to learners myriad subtle, and not so subtle, messages. Indeed, you cannot *not* communicate. You may even communicate if you are not present; frequently arriving late for a class says *something* to your learners.

Unsurprisingly, the theme of effective communication runs throughout the Lifelong Learning UK (LLUK) *Professional standards for teachers, tutors and trainers in the lifelong learning sector*. For example, communication theory and principles appear in Learning and Teaching (Domain B); collaboration and communication with others is included in Professional Values and Practice (Domain A); the importance of feedback appears in Assessment for Learning (Domain E) (LLUK, 2006).

Consequently, communicating with learners forms an important part of the ITT qualifications now on offer. The relevant qualifications are the Certificate in Teaching in the Lifelong Learning Sector (CTLLS) for the associate teacher role, and the Diploma in Teaching in the Lifelong Learning Sector (DTLLS) for the full teaching role. These qualifications are often embedded in university PGCE and Certificate in Education courses. Additionally, effective communication is a relevant topic for the continuing professional development (CPD) of both newly qualified and experienced teachers in the sector.

About this book

Content

Our aim has been to adopt a logical sequence to the content of this book, moving from a general consideration of communication theory to the practical issues you are likely to face in communicating in your professional role as a teacher in the lifelong learning sector. So the book opens with a review of communication theory and how it can be applied in practice (Chapters 2–4). This leads on to a consideration of how communication also has an emotional element which needs to be recognised and may be used to reflect inclusivity and to manage behaviour (Chapters 5–7). The second part of the book concentrates on some specific communication issues within educational organisations: communicating with large groups and with learners at a distance (Chapter 8), communicating within organisations (Chapter 9) and with colleagues (Chapter 10) and finally, a review of resources (Chapter 11).

Structure

All of the chapters in the book, apart from this introduction, follow a similar format and structure that includes:

- links to the LLUK professional standards and to DTLLS and CTLLS mandatory units;
- an introduction that briefly outlines the content of the chapter;
- case studies;
- reflective and practical tasks;
- a summary of the key points covered;
- branching options;
- references and further reading.

The case studies are taken from real-life situations to illustrate the relevant learning points. Many of these case studies are linked to practical and reflective tasks to give you an opportunity to link the content of the book to your own experience. Comments on most of the practical tasks are provided immediately after the task or in the text that follows. In the reflective tasks you are asked to consider certain points, to think about your own experience, or to imagine a situation. There are no correct answers but you might find it useful to record your responses to the tasks.

The branching options at the end of each chapter are designed to help you consolidate and develop what you have learned. These are classified as reflection, analysis and research tasks. The reflection option requires you to think about a particular aspect of the chapter and relate it to your own practice. The analysis option asks you to analyse specific incidents, usually from your own experience, and to relate these to the concepts discussed in the chapter. Finally, the research option gives you the opportunity to explore and develop these concepts in relation to your own professional practice.

There is one final point that we think is important to stress. This book is primarily about you in your professional role as a teacher and, consequently, most of the content focuses on your teaching rather than your learners. We would not wish this emphasis to imply that we are advocating a teacher-centred approach to your role. In fact, the reverse is true. We believe our key role as teachers is to inspire and facilitate learning, in line with Socratic philosophy where *education is the kindling of a flame, not the filling of a vessel*, and this is the basic philosophy of this book. The approach is described in the LLUK standards as follows:

> *The key purpose of the teacher is to create effective and stimulating opportunities for learning through high quality teaching that enables the development and progression of all learners.*
>
> (LLUK, 2006, p2)

To do this effectively, we need to communicate with our learners with skill, empathy and mutual respect. Sometimes this is difficult; learners can be disruptive and antagonistic, resources can be non-existent, colleagues can be uncooperative. We have tried to be realistic in the guidance that we have given in this book, because our experience has taught us that such difficulties are inevitable in a teacher's working life. Nevertheless, we have also found that good communication skills really can help in many of these difficult situations, and getting as far as we can along the road to excellence brings many rewards, both in job satisfaction and in learner experience.

REFERENCES AND FURTHER READING

LLUK (2006) *New overarching professional standards for teachers, tutors and trainers in the lifelong learning sector.* London: LLUK.

Websites

www.lluk.org
www.svuk.eu

2
Communication theory: process, perception and interaction

This chapter will help you to:

- **explore a range of communication theories;**
- **identify the role of perception in communication;**
- **analyse communication transactions;**
- **apply relevant theories of communication to your own teaching.**

Links to LLUK professional standards for QTLS:

AS3, AS4, AS7, AK4.1, AK4.2, AP4.1, AP4.2, AK5.1, AK5.2, AP5.1, AP5.2, BS2, BS3, BK1.2, BP1.2, BK3.1, BK3.3, BK3.4, BP3.1, BP3.3, BP3.4.

Links to CTLLS:

Unit 1 Preparing to teach in the lifelong learning sector;

Unit 2 Planning and enabling learning.

Links to DTLLS:

Unit 1 Preparing to teach in the lifelong learning sector;

Unit 2 Planning and enabling learning;

Unit 4 Theories and principles for planning and enabling learning;

Unit 5 Continuing personal and professional development;

Unit 6 Curriculum development for inclusive practice;

Unit 7 Wider professional practice.

Introduction

If we were to try to imagine life without communicating with each other, apart from the feelings of isolation and loneliness, it would be difficult to imagine how anything would get done. Communicating is central to everything we do; in many ways it's the essence of our humanity. As a species, we communicated even before we were fully human. As individuals, we communicate from the moment we are born (Knapp and Hall, 1992). Indeed, we just do it, without looking too deeply into what *it* actually is.

So, what is communication? Well, when you are reflecting back on a teaching situation, perhaps writing in your reflective journal, you are communicating; in this instance, with yourself (intrapersonal communication). When you smile at a learner you pass in the corridor, you are communicating (interpersonal communication). When you give a lecture or a demonstration you are communicating (group communication).

Almost everything we do in our role as teachers involves some form of communication with our learners, so a good starting point is to consider some theories of communication and then see how they can be applied to improving our day-to-day practice of teaching. So, this chapter begins by looking at why we communicate and then explores some communication models and their relevance for teaching. The second part of the chapter looks at perception and self-image to see how each can influence our interactions with our learners and offers a transactional analysis of communicative interactions.

Why do we communicate?

In *Communication* (1975), Stevens suggests that we use spoken language to:

- obtain something;
- gain information;
- solve a problem;
- inform;
- express our feelings;
- influence and persuade.

If you put this into a typical interaction in your teaching role, you might, for example, ask a learner if their assignment was ready for you to look at (to obtain something). They might tell you that it was, but there was just one small point they were not sure about and needed to ask you (to obtain information). You might make some suggestions (to inform; to solve a problem). You might then say that you are really pleased (or not) with how they are doing (to express our feelings) and encourage them to keep up the good work (influence and persuade).

We also communicate to build and reinforce relationships. This point is worth looking at a little more closely as it is a really important aspect of our teaching role. It has been suggested by Morris (1986) and others, that language has an important role in social bonding. Psychologist Jonathan Haidt (2006) takes up this theme and gives an explanation of one possible reason why we all love to gossip; it actually has a positive effect on social groups.

> *It costs us nothing to give each other information, yet we both benefit by receiving information.*

> (Haidt, 2006, p54)

Haidt goes on to explain that, as social groups increased in size, gossip enabled group members to keep tabs on any members who were no longer in sight. This isn't, of course, a promotion of gossip, but it does suggest that chatting to learners has an important role in our interactions with them.

Communication models

With so many different reasons for communicating, it isn't surprising that when we begin to analyse what is happening, we are faced with quite a complex process. A good way of making this complexity more manageable is to look at some diagrammatical models. Textbooks on communication theory usually include the original Shannon and Weaver linear model and exchange models such as those found in Dimbleby and Burton (1992).

Let me explain the main points of communication theory by introducing you to Arthur and Jasmine. Arthur wants to congratulate Jasmine on her assignment and the interpersonal communication between them could be shown as a diagram:

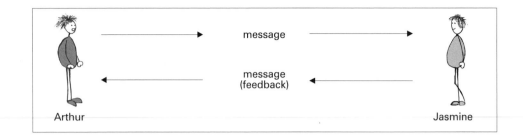

This diagram shows that in any communicative interaction there will be people, messages, and feedback.

People and messages

Communication is an ongoing dynamic process in which two (or more) people send and receive messages. In this case, Arthur has the idea in his mind that he wishes to congratulate Jasmine on her work, and he translates this idea into a message. For example, he could just say, *Well done, Jasmine!* Or he could put his thumbs up as a gesture of congratulation. We use our senses to send and receive messages, so speech, the written word and non-verbal communication are communication channels. A message is represented by symbols that indicate its meaning. Words, pictures and a *thumbs up* gesture are examples of a symbol.

Feedback

Once Jasmine has received the message, she responds to it. She might smile, or say *Thank you*. This response is feedback, and becomes a return message to Arthur. So we now set up a whole process where messages flow back and forth between the two people almost simultaneously. For example, if you are about to speak to a group of learners, you might stand up tall, remain quiet and look around the room at every individual. Your learners will respond to this non-verbal message (*We are about to begin*) by completing their conversations, turning to face you and so on. You will pick up these feedback signals and adjust your response. So, if their feedback indicates that they are ready, you will begin. If it doesn't, you are likely to wait or ask for attention.

Our first diagram is fairly limited for explaining the complexity of communication. In this second diagram I have included a number of other factors that are hugely influential in the process; encoding/decoding, the environment and barriers.

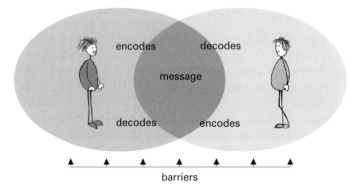

Encoding/decoding

When we are involved in a communicative interaction with another person, each of us has to find a way to give meaning to what we hear and see. We do this by decoding the symbols we receive into a form that makes sense to us. For example, if Arthur did, in fact, say *Congratulations* or make a *thumbs up* gesture, Jasmine would immediately and automatically be able to decode this as, *Arthur is pleased with my work.*

Communication environments

The process of encoding/decoding messages doesn't take place in isolation but within an environment or context. When we talk about environment we are referring to both the physical setting, such as classroom, workplace, sports field, and to the cultural setting, the experience, values, knowledge and expectations of the communicators. So it would be unlikely that Arthur would congratulate Jasmine at a disco, but much more likely that the interaction would be during a classroom session or a tutorial. Nor would Arthur be likely to use a *thumbs up* symbol if he and Jasmine were from Bangladesh or Thailand where this gesture can be interpreted as insulting and obscene.

Environments have an individual and shared element. Your individual environment would be the personal values, knowledge, beliefs and so on that you bring into your teaching. Your shared environment, indicated by the darker shaded segment of the diagram, would be the knowledge and values that you share with your colleagues and learners. So, Arthur is likely to use educational jargon, such as *clear rationale* and *meeting the criteria,* that is generally understood in an educational context, but which an outsider might not understand.

REFLECTIVE TASK

Consider the nature of the communication environment that you share with your colleagues. What assumptions do you make, for example, how you use jargon because of this shared environment?

Barriers

Barrier refers to anything that interferes with the communication process and disrupts or distorts the message. This can happen anywhere in the process, for example, from the moment the message appears as a thought in Arthur's mind to the moment when Jasmine has an identical understanding of it. Barriers can be semantic, physical or psychological (Burton and Dimbleby, 1992). So, let's see how barriers occur.

Semantic barriers

Semantics is concerned with how language communicates meaning. There is potential for a semantic barrier if we use technical or colloquial language without explanation, or we use ambiguous language. For example, in the phrase *when the giants saw the shoes they realised they were too big*, it isn't clear who or what is too big, the giants or the shoes. Other examples of semantic barriers include the degree of formality in our speech, an accent (how we sound when we speak) or a dialect (words and grammar specific to a region).

REFLECTIVE TASK

Can you think of any examples of semantic barriers you have experienced in your teaching role?

Physical barriers

We usually think of physical barriers in terms of background talking or a ringing bell but the meaning is broader and includes, for example, a cold room, a teacher speaking for too long a teacher not focusing on a learner's non-verbal communication (NVC) to check they have understood.

REFLECTIVE TASK

What effect do you think the following physical barriers might have on the communication process: uncomfortable seating, poor lighting?

Psychological barriers

I remember once listening to one of my learners explaining how he planned to tackle an assignment. His explanation wasn't very clear or detailed and I wanted to make sure he understood what he had to do, so I said to him, *Nigel, I'm not sure I understand, could you explain what you mean?* After a thoughtful pause, he replied, *I'm not sure I* know *what I mean*. This was met by hoots of laughter from his fellow learners, but what he'd given was an accurate assessment of his predicament. He was attempting to explain something verbally before it was clear in his mind so, in this instance, his barrier was psychological – faulty encoding. Nigel is not alone. We sometimes speak (and write) before we are sure what we want to say, or we speak with our emotions engaged, for example, when we are feeling irritated, anxious or preoccupied.

REFLECTIVE TASK

What do you think would be the effect on your learners if you spoke to them while you were feeling irritated?

There is further opportunity for psychological barriers to occur in the decoding of any message. Words are arbitrary symbols; they mean *something*, but only because we have agreed that they should. We know that each of us will interpret and understand what we hear and see in a way that makes sense to us. This will mean interpreting messages in the context of our own individual experience and knowledge, in other words according to our own perception. This is almost certain to be different from the perception of the person sending the message, as you will see a little later in this chapter.

Models and their explanations can appear abstract, so let's consider a real-life situation.

> ## CASE STUDY
> **Hannah and Debbie**
>
> Hannah is nearing the end of a Beauty Therapy course. Here she describes an interaction between herself and Debbie, her tutor for one of her modules.
>
> *I was glad to see Debbie in the morning crush as I wanted to give her my assignment. I managed to catch her eye as she was dashing past so I stopped and began to pull my assignment out of my bag. I looked up and started to say,* I've got my H and S, can I give it...? when I realised that she had already passed me, had half-turned back towards me and was glancing at her watch, so I stopped midstream. She said she was in a rush to get to Union, so I told her I'd catch her another time.

PRACTICAL TASK PRACTICAL TASK **PRACTICAL TASK** PRACTICAL TASK **PRACTICAL TASK**

In the above case study can you identify significant features of the communication process in action? What channels are being used? What comments can you make about the encoding process and the environment? What barriers can you identify? Note your response and compare with the following comments.

The first thing to notice about this interaction is that Debbie and Hannah are both actively involved in sending and receiving messages through both verbal and non-verbal channels. Debbie picks up Hannah's non-verbal signals (eye contact, slowing of her pace and fumbling in her bag) as an indication that she wants to talk: this is confirmed by Hannah's words. Hannah picks up Debbie's non-verbal signals (she stopped only after she had already passed, she was turning away and looking at her watch) as an indication that Debbie was short of time and this was confirmed by her words. The second point to notice is that Debbie and Hannah are sending multiple signals (both verbal and non-verbal) and they are sending them almost simultaneously.

There is more we can glean from this illustration. In this interaction Debbie and Hannah are both busy encoding and decoding messages. This process is made much easier and quicker because it takes places within a physical environment that is familiar to them both. When Debbie says that she is on her way to Union, Hannah knows that this means the Union building. They also share a cultural or experiential environment: when Hannah tells Debbie that she has finished her H and S, Debbie knows this means her project on Health and Safety because they both understand the jargon of their shared environment.

There are two potential barriers in this case study. The first is that the interaction between Hannah and Debbie takes place against a busy background (*in the morning crush*). This is a straightforward physical barrier that could disrupt the communication between Hannah and Debbie. The second is the fact that Debbie is in a hurry. She may not listen attentively to what Hannah has to say.

How the process is influenced by perception

Ellis and McClintock (1994) suggest that perception is a vital element of interpersonal communication.

Perception may be regarded as information which is taken in by the senses, processed by the brain, stored in memory and produces some form of physical or mental response.

(Ellis and McClintock, 1994, p1)

To illustrate how we process information taken in by the senses, have a look at the following sign.

**Please keep to the
the inside lane**

Did you notice that the word *the* is repeated in this message? If you didn't, the reason is likely to be that it wouldn't have made sense to you as it stood so you selected, or perceived, only the words that made sense. When I have used a similar example in a class some learners are unable to see the repeated word even when it is pointed out to them. We are not only able to ignore things that don't make sense but to fill in things which we feel should be included, or change things around until they *do* make sense, as in this sentence:

Why deosn't the oredr of the ltteers in this qeusiton mttaer?

(Hall, 2007, p59)

So far, we have looked at how the communication process works and concentrated on how it may be disrupted and distorted by barriers. However, perception has a big role in any communicative interaction. In the context of teaching, perception means how we see learners and ourselves, how our learners see themselves and us, and how we and our learners see the communicative event.

Some aspects of perception

One way to explore perception is to see how it relates to previous experience, to current interactions and to predicting the future.

Previous experience
Many of our perceptions are learned through knowledge and experience gained over our lifetime and through our interactions with those around us. Our culture, our peer group, our family group all play a part in forming values and attitudes which, ultimately, go to form the perceptions that influence our interactions with others. For example, the way we speak to a particular colleague might be influenced by a previous dispute or by an occasion when they were extremely considerate towards us.

Perception is an incredibly individual experience. You could say that each of us views the world around us through our own individual pair of spectacles; these give us a unique viewpoint. For example, what comes into your mind when you see the word *dog*? At first sight, a dog is a dog, is a dog. But your perception of *dog* might be your loving pet waiting at home, a large messy animal that slobbers and leaves muddy footprints, a cute birthday card dog or an animal with large teeth. My perception of *dog* is the last one because I received a nasty bite when I was small.

Current interaction

Our perception of any messages we receive is multi-layered. There is the content element, or factual information contained in the words, usually (but not always) supported by NVC. There is the emotional element, where we judge the other person's emotional state. Most of this information comes via intentional or unintentional NVC. Finally, there is the relationship element where we judge the other person's character, attitudes, the sort of person they are and how we can relate to them, based on what we already know, or think we know, about them.

Expectations for the future

We use our perceptive skills to understand the thoughts and emotions of others in order to plan for the future. We predict what others might say and how they might react to what we say. We also need to plan what we are going to say and are constantly monitoring the feedback we receive in order to adjust and adapt our responses.

To see how perception affects communication we'll return to the interaction between Hannah and Debbie. This time Debbie is speaking.

CASE STUDY

Hannah and Debbie (continued)

I was running a bit late for my team meeting over in Union building when I saw Hannah in the morning crush. She caught my eye and looked really pleased with herself so I knew she wanted to talk, and as soon as she began to search in her bag I knew she was looking for her assignment, and that she intended to hand it in to me. I had to stop and tell her that I was in a rush. Luckily, she'd already got the message because she stopped mid sentence. I don't like taking students' work like this in the corridor. I feel that they put such a lot of effort into their projects and the handover should reflect this. I prefer a few moments, in a quiet place if possible, certainly not in a busy corridor, to check that everything looks to be OK, and that they aren't worried about anything. To be honest, I wasn't running that late and if it had been anyone else I would probably have been tempted to take it because we are a bit behind with the assignments. But I didn't want to begin talking to Hannah, partly because, once she starts, it can be quite difficult to get away, but mainly because she often forgets to do the basic stuff in her assignments, like complete the front sheet. I knew that if I took her assignment I'd only have to give it back to her to fill in the missing bits.

Debbie is approaching this interaction wearing a different set of perceptual spectacles from Hannah. Hannah just wants to get her work in but Debbie has other things to consider; the knowledge that she is running a little late and that Hannah likes to talk, balanced against the knowledge that the assignments are also running late. Debbie's personal values (that learners' work needs to be treated with respect) also come into play, as does the physical environment (it's a crowded corridor, not the best place to talk). Debbie perceives, from Hannah's non-verbal signals (her elated expression and fumbling in her bag) that she has completed her assignment, so she can predict what Hannah is about to say. She also uses knowledge gained from past experience of Hannah (she often hands in incomplete work) to plan what she is going to say.

REFLECTIVE TASK

REFLECTIVE TASK

Think about a recent interaction with one of your learners. Can you identify any of your beliefs or values that you feel influenced your perception of the event? Would you say that it affected your communication with the learner and, if so, how?

Perception and value judgements

Our communication with others is also influenced by how we perceive them and how we see ourselves. Let's look at these two aspects in more detail.

How we see others

When we meet other people we feel more comfortable when we are able to label them from our initial perception of them, and we are actually very skilled at judging from these first impressions. We do it by mentally noting what we see or hear, especially if it is something obvious like a particular dress style, hairstyle or accent. Although it is helpful to have an immediate mental picture of another person, labelling brings its own problems, for example, once we have a particular view of someone, it can be difficult to change the way we see them.

REFLECTIVE TASK

REFLECTIVE TASK

If you were listening to a learner talking about e-communication would it make any difference if the speaker was aged 20 or 60?

Because we view any interaction through our own pair of spectacles we also make value judgements about others that fit our own beliefs and values. We tend to feel that people should be the same as us, have the same values and attitudes and behave in the same way that we do: *Why doesn't she turn the lights off when she has finished?* (*I believe we should conserve energy; she should feel the same way.*) Similarly, *Why does this learner always arrive late?* (*I believe good time keeping is important, she should feel the same way.*)

How we see ourselves

One important component of perception is self-perception or self-image. This refers to our personal understanding of who we are. It is everything we believe about ourselves. It includes our feelings about our physical appearance, our emotional state, our values and attitudes, our skills and talents, our intelligence and so on. Psychologists Combs and Snygg suggest that self-image is:

> ... *essentially a social product arising out of experience with people ... inferences about ourselves made as a consequence of the ways we perceive others behaving towards us.*

> (Combs and Snygg, 1959, cited Adler and Rodman, 2003, p48)

So, our self-image develops from our interactions with people around us, especially those close to us such as parents, teachers, friends and colleagues. As children we may be told that we are talkative, tall, good at drawing and so on. As adults we adjust our self-image as we compare our skills and talents with those of others. On the whole, our self-image remains fairly static but it can be shaken by how others communicate with us. At a meeting I attended recently, I observed a woman approaching one of her colleagues who was perusing a notice board. She greeted him, *Hi, Jim. How are you?* Instead of returning her greeting and saying, *I'll be with you in a moment, I'm just looking to see what's on*, he continued facing the notice board but raised his hand with his index finger pointing to the ceiling to indicate *Wait*!

REFLECTIVE TASK

REFLECTIVE TASK

Imagine you were on the receiving end of this message. How would you feel?

This gesture passed a strong message that Jim didn't value his colleague enough to bother giving a verbal reply. It is likely to have left her feeling uncomfortable and devalued. When our self-image is shaken, it affects our self-esteem. In turn, this can affect the way we communicate with others. Let's return to Debbie and Hannah's interaction in the corridor on a busy morning to see how. We'll speculate and say that Hannah's self-image has been shaken; perhaps her friends get a bit fed up with her because she talks too much and one of them has made a comment. Now read what Hannah has to say about the interaction with Debbie.

CASE STUDY

Hannah and Debbie (continued)

She said, I'm in a rush to get to Union, *but I know she was only saying that as an excuse. I'm sure she did have time to stop and talk, but not with me, so I turned and walked away.*

The comment from Hannah's friend may have damaged her self-esteem. She may be thinking that no one really wants to talk to her. This affects how she interprets Debbie's message and how she responds to it. Now read Debbie's comments about the interaction with Hannah following an episode that has affected *her* self-esteem.

I'd just had a really uncomfortable session with a group of middle managers. I'd worked hard on planning my presentation but they just seemed more interested in pulling it to pieces, and they certainly let me know they weren't impressed. I had to take a minute or two after they left the room just to regain my equilibrium, and this made me a bit late for my team meeting over in Union building. I was feeling pretty sorry for myself. To be honest, what I really wanted was a chance to lick my wounds over a cup of coffee, not attend a team meeting. When Hannah caught my eye I knew she wanted to talk to me. I'd normally be happy to stop and chat, but I just didn't feel like facing anyone, so I told her that I was in a rush.

Debbie's experience with her difficult learners has led her to question her image of herself as a professional. Is she really a bad teacher? So, when Hannah greets her she makes an excuse not to talk.

Transactional analysis

We have another way to analyse interpersonal communication. Transactional Analysis (TA) was originally developed by Eric Berne (1964); it suggests that each of us has three basic selves or ego states – adult, parent and child – and, although we occupy all three, one state usually predominates at any one time.

Ego states

Parent
Our parent ego state is concerned with standards, values and rules, giving instructions and giving information; things our parents told us. (*Don't waste food. Always tell the truth.*) Our parent ego can be controlling and prescriptive (*Don't do that. Try harder*), but also nurturing and supportive (*Well done. It will be OK*).

Child
Our child ego state comes from our experiences as children; it is impulsive, instinctive and emotional. In child ego, we say *I don't care. I don't like. I want!*

Adult
Our adult ego state is detached, logical, reasoning and doesn't judge. It is concerned with asking questions, exploring, analysing, planning and decision-making. In adult we are attentive but calm and we use phrases such as, *Can you explain? Let's see how it works. Let's arrange to meet next Tuesday.*

Have a look at these three tasks to see how this might work in practice. Suggested answers are at the end of the chapter.

PRACTICAL TASK PRACTICAL TASK **PRACTICAL TASK** PRACTICAL TASK **PRACTICAL TASK**

1. You need to tell one of your learners that her assignment falls well short of a pass grade. How might you tell her in parent, child, adult?

2. Decide whether the following statements are in parent or child ego state.

    1 You must get some work done today.

    2 Don't forget to put all your bits and pieces back in the right place when you've finished. Make sure all the pencils go in this drawer and the spare paper goes up here.

    3 I can't deal with this now – I've got too much on my mind!

    4 It's always me that gets the coffee.

    5 Don't stand in the way. They can't see.

3. Rewrite each of the above statements in adult ego.

Transactions

In our interactions with others, our ego state (parent, child or adult) will interact with the ego state of the other person. These interactions, or transactions as Berne called them, can be either complementary or crossed.

Complementary transactions
Complementary ego states are: adult to adult, parent to parent, child to child, child to parent and parent to child.

In this example, adult ego addresses adult ego.

This book on Shakespeare is really interesting.
And the response is also adult ego to adult ego.
I agree. I thoroughly enjoyed it.

In this example, parent addresses parent.
They should do something about this equipment. It's getting too old to be of any use.
And the response is also parent to parent.
I know, I'm always having problems with it.

In this example, child addresses child.
Let's have another coffee. I'm sure we've got time.
And the response is child to child.
We'll make time, and what about another biscuit?

In this example, child addresses parent.
Shall we have another coffee? Do you think we have time?
And the response is parent to child.
We don't really have time but, OK, go on then.

Crossed transactions

In a crossed transaction the responder doesn't respond in an ego state that matches the initial statement. Some crossed transactions can result in conflict.

In this example, parent addresses child.
You need to listen more carefully.
But the response is parent to child (rather than child to parent).
And you need to speak more slowly.

Other crossed transactions can resolve conflict.

In this example, parent addresses child.
You need to listen more carefully.
But the response is adult to adult.
You are right. It would help me if you could speak more slowly.

Byrne suggested that some transactions involve games. Here is an example of a *game*.

CASE STUDY

It won't work

You are in the staff room having a well-earned coffee. One of your colleagues is having problems with the photocopier. Some paper has jammed and she can't figure out where. She appeals to you for help.

Colleague: *The paper has jammed. Any ideas?*
You: *The problem might be in the feeder tray.*
Colleague: *No, I've looked there.*
You: *Let's work back from the other end.*
Colleague: *No, that's no good.*

> You: *Well, perhaps we should get the technician to sort it.*
>
> Colleague: *Oh, he's never around when you need him.*
>
> In this scenario you are never going to be able to help your colleague solve the problem of the photocopier because she is not interested in finding a solution. And this is the game she plays; asking for help that she doesn't want.

TA is useful for exploring our interactions because it gives us tools to reflect on specific interactions, to recognise which ego state we occupy and to work towards giving the adult ego state a bigger role in our communication.

Applying theory in your teaching

So, what's the point of including a chapter on communication theory? I believe that any theory has value only if we can use it in practice. If this is true, what can we draw from our review of communication theory that will help us in communicating with our learners? I think it gives us some important precepts that we can relate to our teaching.

- Each of us brings our own environment to any interaction. This means that learners will not necessarily see things the same way as we do because the starting point of their interactions with us is their own values and beliefs. Nor do they necessarily expect or want the same outcome from any interaction with us.
- There is a wide range of barriers that can disrupt communication. These include psychological barriers such as differences in perception, low self-esteem, labelling, etc., semantic barriers, such as jargon, and physical barriers, such as background noise or a learner with poor vision. It is useful for us to be able to recognise potential barriers specific to our teaching role.
- We have an opportunity through our communication to build self-esteem in our learners and enhance their learning experience.

We will explore all of these issues in greater depth in the chapters that follow.

A SUMMARY OF **KEY POINTS**

> The process of communication involves people, messages, channels, symbols and feedback.

> Sender and receiver are both active in the process and will send and receive multiple messages more or less simultaneously.

> Communication takes place within individual and shared environments.

> Communication is effective when messages are not distorted or disrupted by barriers.

> Perception, self-image and self-esteem play an important role in communication.

> Transactional analysis can give us insight into our communicative interactions.

Branching options

The following tasks are designed to help you consolidate and develop your understanding of the process of communication.

Reflection

Consider your experience at work over the recent past to identify any incidents that you feel have affected your self-image. Has this influenced how you communicate with others? How?

Analysis

In one of your next lessons, make a note of any occasion where a communication problem arises. For example, it could be that your learners don't understand one of your instructions, or that you misunderstand what one of your learners is trying to say. After the lesson, try to analyse the problem in relation to the communication process outlined in this chapter.

Research

Search the literature and the internet for models of communication. You will doubtless come across Lasswell, Shannon and Weaver, Schramm and Osgood and several more. Choose one model that you feel is appropriate to your teaching and apply it to a segment of one of your classes. Note how the model is relevant to any significant incident that occurs during the lesson.

Suggested answers to practical tasks, page 14
Task 1
Parent: *This is very poor. I expected much better of you.*
Child: *I can't mark this.*
Adult: *We need to work out where things went wrong.*

Task 2
1 Parent;
2 Parent;
3 Child:
4 Child;
5 Parent.

Task 3
1 *It's time to begin work.*
2 *Please make sure everything is put away when you've finished.*
3 *I'm really tied up at the moment. Could we sort this out later?*
4 *I'd like us to have a rota for the coffee.*
5 *Could you move to one side so everyone can see?*

REFERENCES AND FURTHER READING

Adler, B and Rodman, G (2003) *Understanding Human Communication.* Oxford: Oxford University Press.

Berne, E (1964) *Games people play; the psychology of human relationships.* New York: Ballantine Books.

Burton, G and Dimbleby, R (1992) *More than words: an introduction to communication.* London: Routledge.

Ellis, R and McClintock, A (1994) *If you take my meaning: theory into practice in human communication.* London: Edward Arnold.

Haidt, J (2006) *The happiness hypothesis: putting ancient wisdom and philosophy to the test of modern science.* London: William Heinemann.

Hall, S (2007) *This means that: a user's guide to semiotics.* London: Lawrence King Publishing Ltd.

Knapp, M L and Hall, J A (1992) *Nonverbal communication in human interaction*. Orlando, Florida: Harcourt Brace Jovanovich.

Morris, D (1986) *The naked ape.* London: Jonathan Cape.

Stevens, R (1975) Unit 7: Interpersonal communication, in Open University (ed) *Communication*. Buckingham: Open University Press.

Websites

www.itaa-net.org

3
Listening and speaking skills

This chapter will help you to:

- use your listening and speaking skills more effectively;
- apply these skills to explaining, questioning and advising.

Links to LLUK professional standards for QTLS:

AS3, AS4, AS7, AK4.2, AP4.2, AK5.1, AP5.1, BS2, BS3, BK1.2, BP1.2, BK3.1, BK3.2, BK3.3, BK3.4, BP3.1, BP3.2, BP3.3, BP3.4, EK4.1, EP4.1.

Links to CTLLS:

Unit 1 Preparing to teach in the lifelong learning sector;

Unit 2 Planning and enabling learning.

Links to DTLLS:

Unit 1 Preparing to teach in the lifelong learning sector;

Unit 2 Planning and enabling learning;

Unit 4 Theories and principles for planning and enabling learning;

Unit 5 Continuing personal and professional development.

Introduction

Speaking and listening is by far the most widespread form of communication even in the most literate person's life. In most jobs people spend much more time speaking, listening and discussing than reading or writing.

(DfES, 2001, p20)

Having considered some communication theory, let's now see how this can be applied to the practical skills of communication in our role as teachers. Much of the literature on communication identifies four basic skills – speaking, listening, reading and writing – but I think we should add NVC to this list. In this chapter we will look at listening and speaking and explore some of the barriers that can interfere with the process; in the following chapter the focus will be on NVC and written communication.

Listening

You might expect a chapter on practical communication skills to begin with speaking rather than listening. After all, speaking takes up a good proportion of teacher time. But we listen more than we speak, and listening is also one of the most important communication skills; you could say that a good communicator is very likely to be a good listener (Wallace, 2007).

There are three things to think about when we look at the process of listening: we need to be able to hear, we need to actively listen and we need to understand.

Hearing

Obviously, we need to be able to hear what learners say to us. But in many teaching situations this isn't always so easy in practice. I expect you can think of occasions when you have battled against a variety of background noise; passing traffic, noisy machinery or just enthusiastic learners in adjacent classes. There probably isn't too much we can do about this apart from being flexible and changing our routine. A DTLLS trainee told me recently that he works in an open access area with a constant flow of learners en route to and from a resources section at the back. It is almost impossible for anyone to hear properly so he has decamped to a nearby vacant office.

A little closer to home, you may well have one or two people in your group who feel the need to speak when everyone is trying to hear what a learner is saying. It just doesn't work, of course, and it's unfair to expect anyone to continue speaking against background noise, so everyone needs to know that chatter is not appropriate when someone is speaking.

Sometimes learners who are feeling nervous will speak hesitantly, or speak softly or quickly. We can certainly ask them to speak a little louder or a little slower although, hopefully, not follow this example I observed recently at a local history class I attend. On this particular occasion, the teacher asked the class if there were any questions and a fellow learner said there was something that was bothering her. She began her question a little tentatively, possibly to give herself time to think of the best way to phrase it. Before she had uttered more than a couple of words, the teacher interrupted her to say, rather loudly, *Speak up, we can't hear you.*

REFLECTIVE TASK

Imagine you were this learner. How would you understand this instruction? How would you feel?

This instruction contained two messages. The first was an overt request; the learner was being asked to speak up. The delivery of the message (rather loudly) was hardly sensitive and likely to make her feel uncomfortable. But there was also a covert message; the teacher used the word *we* rather than *I*, so the learner would feel that it wasn't only the teacher who couldn't hear her but the whole class. If no one in the class could hear, this was probably worse in the learner's estimation than if it were just the teacher. The learner's non-verbal reaction to this instruction was exactly as you would expect. She was embarrassed. Her verbal response was, *Oh! It's OK. It doesn't matter – I've sorted it.* She hadn't.

You might be tempted to think that it was acceptable for the teacher to speak this way. After all, you can't wrap people in cotton wool. But it's not; apart from being insensitive, we can't afford to communicate in any way that prevents a learner from speaking.

Listening

Of course we listen to learners; or do we?

PRACTICAL TASK   PRACTICAL TASK   PRACTICAL TASK   PRACTICAL TASK   PRACTICAL TASK

Wherever you are reading this book, stop. Close your eyes and, for at least 30 seconds, just listen to the sounds around you. What do you hear?

You may have heard people talking, humming machinery, such as a computer, a ticking clock, the sound of wind, traffic noise, a passing plane, birdsong. Are you surprised at the number and variety of sounds around you? If you did this task indoors it's worth repeating it outside. One other thing you might have noticed in this task is that listening requires a certain amount of concentration. To actively listen, you need to make an effort. The chances are that, before doing the practical task, you weren't aware of the majority of the sounds you heard. Our senses are constantly bombarded with stimuli. We only manage this massive input of information because we are able to block out anything we don't need to hear. This ability makes it very easy for us to switch off.

Listening is one of the most highly valued management skills (Adler and Rodman, 2003). It's easy to see why. If you don't listen properly you are unlikely to be able to anticipate and deal with any problems. Poor listening also impacts on relationships. It tells the speaker that you don't value what they are saying. Actively listening, on the other hand, tells the speaker that what they have to say is important to you. Yet, despite this, on the whole, we're not all that good at it. This isn't too surprising really because good listening is a skill: to do it well you need to learn to do it and to practise.

So what goes wrong? Why do we sometimes fail to listen properly? There is an uncomfortably long list of reasons, but first, let's observe an interaction between a teacher and a learner where one or two things have gone wrong.

CASE STUDY
Nobody listens!

George has been attending a GCSE geography class for a number of weeks. He hasn't found it all that easy and admits he doesn't overwork himself, preferring evenings at the pub rather than at the grindstone. But he has managed to keep going and to keep his head above water – just. He arrives for his Monday morning class feeling unusually optimistic. There is a reason for his optimism. Everyone has been asked to find out something about Australasia for this morning's class. Just by chance, in the pub last night, a guy was going on about the time he'd lived in Sydney and George thinks he has picked up a thing or two that will stand him in good stead for this morning.

Nick, the teacher, gets the class to work in small groups with the intention of feeding back to the whole class at the end. George has the biggest input in his group (thanks to the guy in the pub) and, unusually, offers to be spokesperson. At the end of the discussion Nick stops the groups and asks for the name of each spokesperson. When George's name comes up, Nick gives him a long look but says nothing. He then asks for the feedback from each group, during which he frequently glances at his watch. Time is fast running out when Nick gets to the final group, George's, so he tells George that he must sum up their discussion in one short sentence. Dismayed, George does his best to get as much information as he can into his one sentence, whereupon Nick gives him another long look but says only, *Thank you, George,* and immediately launches into a set of instructions concerning the forthcoming mock exam. George leaves the class thinking, *What's the point of doing any work anyway – nobody listens.*

Was Nick listening? If you feel he wasn't, what reasons would you suggest for his failure? Note your response and compare with the comments below.

Nick wasn't listening, at least not to George, and there are three reasons or barriers that interfered with his listening. First, he judged and labelled George; second, he was thinking about something else; third, he was rehearsing what he was going to say. Let's take these in turn.

- Nick made a judgement about George's knowledge of the subject. This is a good example of how we all make value judgements based on past experience. He used his experience over the previous weeks to label George as a learner with little of worth to say. His first long look at George may well have been a message to this effect. He decided to leave George's group until last; you can almost hear his thoughts, *Well, I won't get much from that group today; not with George taking the lead. I'll leave them until last in case we run out of time.* He is probably taken aback by George's knowledgeable summing up of the group's work (hence the second long look), but time is short and it is now too late to do anything about it. We all make judgements when we listen to learners: we may believe they are not sure of their facts, or that they wouldn't know too much about a particular topic.
- Nick was thinking about the time and the fact that he had information to pass on to the class. Again, this was communicated non-verbally (glancing at his watch). This, too, is something we have all done, pretending to listen when we are really thinking about something we have forgotten to do or the pile of assignments waiting to be looked at.
- Nick was rehearsing what he was going to say to the class. We don't know this for sure but it's likely that the information on the mock exam was important and the learners needed to be clear about what was expected of them. We saw in Chapter 2 that planning our responses is a normal part of communication, but too much planning is a barrier to listening.

Here are some more reasons why we don't always listen.

- We are not interested, or interested only in some of what's being said. A learner is telling us about his enthusiasm for motor racing. It's a bore, so we politely pretend to listen.
- We don't agree with, or don't like, what is being said. A colleague has strong political views. We don't share them so we tune out.
- We think we already know what the speaker is saying. Perhaps a learner is explaining a point. We've heard this point many times before so we switch off. We are experts at pretend listening.
- We prefer to talk. We actually like talking much more than we like listening, and find giving information and advice much more rewarding. The danger signs to look for are when we feel we have something we really need to say or we know *exactly* the advice we need to give.

Nick, in the above case study, is not alone. Very few of us are naturally effective listeners. To be effective your listening needs to be active. There are several aspects to active listening.

- Be open to what learners have to say. Don't have expectations about what they are going to say or make judgements about their knowledge or interest in the topic. I once heard this attitude described as interacting with others *as if for the first time*; in other words, as if you know nothing about them so have no expectations. This isn't always easy, especially with some learners, and takes practice but it is worth the effort.
- Be aware of the learner's NVC. If Nick had taken note of George's NVC he would have seen him fidgeting on his seat, looking around expectantly as he waited for his turn to amaze the class with his extensive

knowledge. When asked to limit his report to one short sentence, George's expression of dismay, and perhaps confusion or hostility, would have been obvious. More of this in the following chapter.

- Give verbal and non-verbal feedback. Verbal feedback includes words and phrases such as, *I see. Go on. Yes.* Non-verbal feedback includes smiling, maintaining eye contact and nodding when appropriate. Feedback encourages the speaker to continue and makes them feel that their contribution is valued.
- Don't be in a hurry. Give learners time to speak and don't interrupt if you can avoid it.
- Ask questions. Questioning gives the learner an opportunity to expand and clarifies certain points for you and the rest of the class. More on this later.
- Paraphrase the learner's words. Paraphrasing means conveying the meaning of something using different words. It shows the speaker that you are listening. McKay et al (2009) give a number of reasons why paraphrasing is so valuable in listening and I have listed some of them here.
  - People really appreciate feeling heard.
  - Paraphrasing allows false assumptions, errors and misinterpretations to be corrected.
  - Paraphrasing makes it more difficult to compare, judge, rehearse what you want to say or advise.
  - It helps you to remember what has been said.

PRACTICAL TASK PRACTICAL TASK **PRACTICAL TASK** PRACTICAL TASK **PRACTICAL TASK**

With a friend or colleague, take turns paraphrasing each other's words. Begin with a short sentence and gradually increase the amount you say as you get more used to it. Try to get across the whole meaning of your partner's message using your own words. Give critical feedback to each other.

A few weeks ago I observed an interaction between a teacher and a learner. The learner had chosen an inappropriate moment (the teacher was having lunch with colleagues in a college refectory) to approach her with a query about his assignment. The teacher suggested to the learner that they deal with it another time. But what was interesting about this interaction was the teacher's NVC. Firstly, she gave the learner her full attention (she turned away from her colleagues, looked straight at him and smiled) to show that she was ready to listen to him. Secondly, she spoke warmly and used the tone of her voice to convey to the learner that his problem was important to her. This interaction took less than 20 seconds (no longer than it would have taken whatever she might have decided to say in response to his query), but the learner went away feeling that he'd really been listened to.

PRACTICAL TASK PRACTICAL TASK **PRACTICAL TASK** PRACTICAL TASK **PRACTICAL TASK**

Stand in front of a mirror and say the phrase *We've run out of time but we'll sort this out tomorrow* out loud as if you are:

- really interested;
- short of time;
- thinking about something else.

Note the change in your expression and your voice.

To indicate interest, you are likely to have focused on your reflection, leaned forward slightly, used a supportive tone and probably emphasised the words *sort* and *tomorrow*. To indicate shortness of time, you may have dropped your eye contact with your reflection, shaken your head slightly and spoken more rapidly. To indicate that you were thinking about something else you may have looked away and used a dismissive hand gesture.

Understanding

Let's assume that we are able to hear our learners perfectly and we are expert listeners. This would appear to be a recipe for success, but we are not quite there yet. There is the final stage in the communication process where the message is received and de-coded. We need to understand what the speaker, in our case a learner, wants to say to us. Here are two reasons why this may not happen.

- There is a language difference. I am not talking here about an actual language difference, such as English/ French, but about the language differences in spoken English. The comment attributed to George Bernard Shaw that *the English and the Americans are peoples divided by a common language* highlights this. Some of our learners will speak a different language. We need to be aware that each learner has a unique language profile, a product of their cultural and educational background. Some might use jargon and slang that we think we understand, but don't. Others might use a dialect containing words that we may interpret incorrectly as far as their intended meaning is concerned.
- We may not interpret the whole message. We saw in Chapter 2 that we use both verbal and non-verbal channels to send our messages. Words convey much of our factual message but the majority of our emotions and feelings are conveyed non-verbally. We will deal with NVC in more depth later, but it's worth noting here that there are many opportunities in teaching for us to misunderstand a learner's message because we failed to observe, or to interpret correctly, its non-verbal component. A learner may tell us that he is bored with something he is being asked to do, but his non-verbal cues (frown, unhappy expression) might be saying he is feeling pretty uncomfortable and unhappy because he doesn't understand what is expected of him.

Speaking

In teaching we do a lot of speaking; there is usually a lot that needs to be said. Even with the variety of learner-centred teaching strategies available to us, speaking to learners is still one of the mainstays of teaching. It makes sense then to spend some time thinking about how we go about it. So, let's begin this section on speaking by looking at a couple of practical problems experienced by two lecturers, Ian and Helen, who are both working towards a DTLLS qualification. Firstly Ian:

I'm a catering lecturer in a Further Education college. One difficulty I have with talking to my students is the actual arrangement of the kitchen. We are housed in an old building that was never intended to be used as a kitchen, certainly not a teaching kitchen. It has lots of nooks and crannies and this makes it difficult for me to speak to the whole class. There are always some students who can neither see nor hear me properly.

Now Helen:

I teach beauty therapy in the same college as Ian. My problem is very different. I am from Yorkshire and I have a typical Yorkshire accent. In my group I have some students from Eastern Europe and they have great difficulty understanding my pronunciation, especially the e vowels. It makes communicating with them very difficult. Luckily, my other students are very helpful and will repeat the problem words.

Ian and Helen's experiences bring us right back to two communication fundamentals. In order to learn effectively from what we say, learners need to be able to hear (and preferably see) us, and they need to be able to understand us.

Hearing and understanding

Let's look at a situation where some learners don't hear the teacher because he positively discourages them from listening.

CASE STUDY

Can't stand the heat!

It is a warm day at the end of the summer term. Dave needs to give his NVQ apprentices information about their final assessment. The workshop has floor-to-ceiling windows along one side and, although the glass is tinted, it soon becomes very warm as the sun reaches that side of the building. Soon the learners start to fidget and one or two ask for time out for a quick drink. At the back of the group, two or three are muttering to each other. Dave is aware that they are hot but he only has today to give out this information. There are just half a dozen points left on his list and he reckons it will only take another fifteen minutes, so he battles on to the bitter end.

PRACTICAL TASK PRACTICAL TASK **PRACTICAL TASK** PRACTICAL TASK **PRACTICAL TASK**

Was Dave right to carry on *to the bitter end*? What other course of action was open to him? Note your response and compare with the comments below.

I expect you can understand Dave's dilemma. You've probably been in a similar situation, where time is short but there are things that you need to tell your learners. It's tempting to carry on even when you become aware that you have lost them. Dave's learners are unlikely to be listening; they are more concerned with getting out of the workshop and getting a drink, and the muttering at the back would have made it difficult to hear anyway. Here are a couple of general points from Dave's experience.

- Any sort of discomfort, for example a room that is too hot or too cold, uncomfortable chairs, poor lighting, background noise and so on, is likely to discourage learners from listening even if they are able to hear what you say.
- There are limits to learners' concentration spans even when they are physically comfortable, so giving too much information in one go is counterproductive.

Let's now consider a situation where the teacher has made it almost impossible for a learner to understand what he is saying.

CASE STUDY

I didn't quite catch that!

Julie has just retired from work as a senior retail manager and has decided to do some of the things that her busy and demanding working life hadn't allowed her to do. She wants to improve her digital imaging skills so she has enrolled for a course at the local college. Her first lesson passed pretty well. Hamid, her teacher, showed everyone what to do and she has managed to produce some good results. Julie is working through a worksheet on her second session when she hits a problem, so she asks for help. Hamid listens to her problem and fixes things straight away. Julie, who has spent all her working life solving problems, needs to know what she can do if the problem

---

recurs. *Well, that's easy,* says Hamid, and immediately reels off half a dozen instructions in rapid succession in some sort of computerspeak, which Julie believes must be from one of the outer planets of the solar system, before disappearing to help someone else.

PRACTICAL TASK PRACTICAL TASK **PRACTICAL TASK** PRACTICAL TASK **PRACTICAL TASK**

If you were watching this interaction, what advice might you give to Hamid? Note your response and compare with the comments below.

You would probably have suggested that Hamid could do some, or all, of the following.

- Take things more slowly and don't overload the learner with information. He spoke far too quickly and gave too much information in one go for Julie to pick up anything worthwhile.
- Avoid unnecessary jargon and explain difficult words. Be sensitive to learners' background knowledge and general level of understanding. We know our subject in depth. We are familiar with its vocabulary and its technical words. Learners aren't. They sometimes don't understand words that most teachers use on a day-to-day basis. For example, Petty (2009, p41) quotes about twenty such words that learners with A–C GCSE grades did not understand, including *define, analyse, postpone, deduce* and *facilitate.*
- Suggest that Julie writes some notes to remind herself what to do. The action of writing helps many learners to remember.
- Check that Julie has understood by taking time to ask her, instead of rushing off.

Three aspects of our use of language can prevent a learner understanding what we say: ambiguous words, imprecise language and idiom.

Ambiguous words
Words such as *often, sometimes, large* and *likely*, where meaning depends on comparison, are always problematic. For example, does *sometimes* mean every week, every day or every half hour? We have *many* (another ambiguous word) such words in our language. It would make life difficult if we avoided using them completely. It's better to be aware of when you are likely to use them and clarify them.

Imprecise language
Learners will find it easier to understand you if your language is precise. For example, *You need to complete this in twenty minutes* is more precise than *You need to complete this as quickly as possible.*

Idiom
Idiom is a handy shortcut for conveying meaning. Examples include *get your skates on* (hurry up) and *take five* (take a quick break). You might expect learners to be as familiar with idiom as you are, but it isn't necessarily so. Learners from other parts of the UK might be unfamiliar with local idiom and learners from outside the UK, and learners with autism are likely to be completely baffled, so it's best to limit its use and always explain its meaning.

REFLECTIVE TASK

Try to become aware of when you use idiom. Become aware of when others around you use it. You may be surprised at how big a part it plays in spoken language.

Applying speaking and listening skills

It is a statement of the obvious to say that we listen and speak pretty much all the time when we are communicating with our learners. But I think it's useful to look at one or two specific situations to illustrate how we can apply the general points of good practice that we have just covered. Let's look at explaining, questioning and advising.

Explaining

Learners need to feel confident that they know what is expected of them. I remember an occasion when I was a learner, where the maths teacher had explained to the class what we were supposed to do to solve an equation but I hadn't understood. I can remember feeling uncomfortable, embarrassed and anxious because I believed that my fellow learners would all be able to complete the task and I would be shown up. I also remember frantically looking around the room at the other learners to see if I could work out what I should be doing. You might find the following points helpful to prevent this sort of scenario.

- Carefully explain intended goals and targets at the beginning of the session, how the session will be organised and what you expect of the learners. You need to be organised and clear in your own mind about what you want them to do or understand. Structure your explanation with key words to signpost the content and keep it as concise as you can.
- Paraphrasing important points is also helpful. We often gain a better understanding when an explanation is repeated in a slightly different way.
- Check that everyone understands, bearing in mind that not all learners will respond to, *Does everyone understand?* If you are not confident that everyone is happy about what to do, try something like, *There was quite a lot there. I think it's a good idea if I go over it again.* You can also back up with handouts or key points on a board or flip-chart.

REFLECTIVE TASK

In one of your next teaching sessions, make a point of observing the learners following your explanation of a task they are to undertake. What messages are there on how the learners might be feeling? Are they interested, excited, bored, puzzled or something else? Consider the possible reasons for this.

Asking questions

We ask questions:

- to find out what a learner already knows;
- to check understanding;
- to encourage learners to think about the topic.

There are two types of questions we use in teaching – closed questions and open questions. Closed questions require only a *yes* or *no* answer or a short, usually factual, answer. Some examples are: *Do you understand? What is the capital of Scotland?* Open questions encourage learners to speak. Some examples are: *What do you know about...? What would you do if...?* Closed questions have a limited use in teaching. Open questions are more effective for encouraging learners to think and to engage in discussion.

Here are some things to think about when asking questions.

- You need to have everyone's attention. Some teachers prefer to ask a general question to the whole class. I prefer to ask individual learners unless I have someone in the group who is anxious about speaking. People will often not respond to a general question, preferring instead to wait for someone else to answer. A few learners will never volunteer unless asked individually. Once they get into the habit of not answering it is almost impossible for them to change. One way round this difficulty is to pose the question to the whole class, pause so that all the learners have a chance to think about a response, and then nominate an individual learner to answer. When I was training as a teacher, this technique was known as PPP or *pose, pause, pounce*!
- Make sure your question is clear and specific and ask only one question at a time.
- Observe the learner's NVC. Frowns, fidgeting and lack of eye contact can indicate discomfort or confusion. You might need to repeat the question or check that they understand it.
- Use open and closed questions appropriately and try to increase your use of open questions.
- Give learners time to think about answering. Don't interrupt unless you really have to and don't be tempted to finish an answer.
- Use verbal and non-verbal cues such as *yes, go on*, eye contact and nods appropriately to encourage learners to speak.
- Value every answer. This doesn't mean you shouldn't correct wrong answers. Corrections need to be short and clear and then give praise. You can either find something in the answer to praise or you can give praise because the learner had a good go at answering. You can also use phrases such as *That's a really good start, can you say more about it?* Valuing learners' answers helps to build self-confidence, not only for the learner answering; others will take note and feel more confident about contributing.
- Don't allow other learners to make negative comments.

Answering questions

One anxiety that many newly qualified teachers have is connected to their knowledge of their subject. They worry that learners will ask a question, they won't know the answer and their ignorance will be on show for everyone to see. It can be a worry when a learner asks you a question and you don't know the answer but don't panic. Don't be tempted to bluff your way through; this seldom works. Remember, you don't *have* to know every answer, no teacher can know everything. Just stay calm, say that you don't know but you will find out and get back to them. You might also ask the group to see whether they can find the answer. Occasionally, a learner will use questions to derail you from your topic. Always acknowledge their questions but don't get sidetracked.

Here are a couple of points to think about when answering learners' questions.

- Listen carefully to the question and show that you are listening.
- Don't interrupt. Even if you know what question you are being asked, don't be tempted to finish the sentence for them.
- If you can't hear or don't understand the question, ask the learner to repeat it.
- Repeat the question aloud so that everyone in the room has a chance to hear it.

Advising

There are occasions in teaching when we need to offer advice and support to individual learners. It isn't always easy to know the best communicative approach.

CASE STUDY

I don't know what to say!

Rachel is a newly qualified teacher. She enjoys her role teaching level 2 Horticulture but is worried. It is the lunch break and Sue, a more experienced colleague, sees her worried look and asks what's wrong.

Rachel explains that she is worried about a tutorial she has with Sophie, one of her learners, later in the day. She tells Sue that Sophie is very behind in her assignment. When she'd previously asked Sophie why her work wasn't in, Sophie had told her she'd got into a mess with it. She couldn't work out the order, everything was spread out on the carpet but she couldn't face doing it. And anyway, she had too many other things to worry about. She had lost her part-time job and the landlord was making things difficult with the rent. Rachel had listened to Sophie's problems but felt that she'd not been any help at all and they'd done nothing about the assignment. Now she had to face Sophie again and she didn't know what to say.

PRACTICAL TASK PRACTICAL TASK **PRACTICAL TASK** PRACTICAL TASK **PRACTICAL TASK**

If you were Sue, what could you say to Rachel to help her with the forthcoming tutorial with Sophie? Note your response and compare with the comments below.

You might begin by telling Rachel that she was approaching the problem in the right way. She was thinking about how she was going to tackle it and planning ahead. She would probably find it helpful to jot down a number of things she wanted to achieve in the forthcoming tutorial and a few questions she might ask Sophie.

It goes without saying that Rachel should be friendly and reassuring in her approach, give Sophie her full attention, to encourage her to speak and to listen carefully. She was probably doing all this anyway. In fact it sounds as if Rachel has already listened to Sophie's problems and this, in itself, may well have helped Sophie. However, there are two separate problems here, the problem of the assignment and the problem of the rent, and the way Rachel communicates with Sophie will be different for each.

Because Sophie has confided in Rachel, she has placed her in the position of informal counsellor. But Rachel is not a counsellor and she can only deal with this in one way: to listen and to show Sophie that she understands her worries. She can do this by paraphrasing Sophie's words, *I know this is really worrying you*, and offering words of support: *We have advisers who can help you work out the best thing to do.* She can't advise Sophie herself, only refer her to a professional in the organisation's support service.

The problem with the assignment is different. Sophie needs to get up to date and Rachel's role is twofold. Firstly, she needs to let Sophie know that she understands her anxieties about the assignment. Sophie might have already managed to get on with it but if she is still struggling, Rachel needs to acknowledge Sophie's worries, *I know you are really struggling with this,* and encourage her not to give up, *but it can be sorted out*. She can then give Sophie some suggestions as to how the assignment can be tackled. Rachel and Sophie can then come to an agreement about what Sophie is going to do and what Rachel is happy with.

The general points here can be applied to nearly all one-to-one communication situations with learners, and can be summarised as a professional approach that encompasses the following.

- Plan your approach and be clear about what you wish to attain from the interaction.
- Prepare the environment (furniture, room layout, etc.) to encourage interaction.
- Be welcoming and encouraging, with the appropriate listening skills.
- Acknowledge learners' anxieties and show support.
- Be aware of your limits and boundaries.

A SUMMARY OF **KEY POINTS**

> **Listen actively to learners to make sure you hear and understand them correctly. Active listening includes: being open (not making judgements or having expectations); giving appropriate feedback; being aware of the speaker's NVC; asking questions and paraphrasing.**

> **Try to sort out any physical barriers such as background noise or a cold room.**

> **When speaking to learners, speak clearly, use appropriate language and avoid culturally specific language, jargon or idiom. Structure your speech with key words to reinforce important points and to direct the listeners. Don't overload learners with too much information and don't speak for too long.**

> **When asking questions, try to increase your use of open questions, and use verbal and non-verbal cues to encourage learners to speak and to show you value every answer.**

> **When answering questions, listen carefully to the question, if necessary repeat it and, if you don't know the answer, say that you will find out.**

> **In a tutorial situation or when advising a learner, be clear what you wish to attain, be welcoming and supportive but know your limits and boundaries.**

Branching options

The following tasks are designed to help you consolidate and develop your skills of listening and speaking.

Reflection

Consider one of your recent lessons to identify any barriers that affected the way you listened to your learners. Consider how these barriers could be avoided or diminished in future lessons.

Analysis

Try to arrange for one of your lessons to be videoed or observed by a colleague. Analyse your technique for posing and responding to questions. To what extent do you meet the criteria for effective questioning given in this chapter?

Research

Revisit the theories of the communication process that were discussed in Chapter 2, particularly concerning barriers to effective communication. Use the literature to evaluate the extent to which these barriers can disrupt the speaking and listening process, and illustrate this by reference to your own teaching experience.

REFERENCES AND FURTHER READING

Adler, B and Rodman, G (2003) *Understanding Human Communication.* Oxford: Oxford University Press.

Appleyard, N and Appleyard, K (2009) *The Minimum Core for Language and Literacy: knowledge, understanding and personal skills*. Exeter: Learning Matters.

DfES (2001) *Adult literacy core curriculum*. London: DfES.

Ellis, R and McClintock, A (1994) *If you take my meaning: theory and practice in human communication*. London: Edward Arnold.

McKay, M, Davis, M and Fanning, P (1983) *Messages: the communication skills book*. Oakland, CA: New Harbinger Publications.

Petty, G (2009) *Teaching Today*. Cheltenham: Stanley Thornes Ltd.

Stenstrom, A (1996) *An introduction to spoken interaction*. Harlow: Longman.

Wallace, S (2007) *Teaching, tutoring and training in the lifelong learning sector*. Exeter: Learning Matters.

4

Non-verbal communication, writing and reading skills

This chapter will help you to:

- **recognise and understand NVC;**
- **write effectively for your learners;**
- **develop your reading skills;**
- **give appropriate feedback to learners.**

Links to LLUK professional standards for QTLS:

AS3, AS4, AS7, AK4.2, AP4.2, AK5.1, AP5.1, BS2, BS3, BK1.2, BP1.2, BK3.1, BK3.3, BK3.4, BP3.1, BP3.3, BP3.4, ES4, EK4.1, EP4.1.

Links to CTLLS:

Unit 1 Preparing to teach in the lifelong learning sector;

Unit 2 Planning and enabling learning;

Unit 3 Principles and practice of assessment.

Links to DTLLS:

Unit 1 Preparing to teach in the lifelong learning sector;

Unit 2 Planning and enabling learning;

Unit 3 Enabling learning and assessment;

Unit 4 Theories and principles for planning and enabling learning;

Unit 5 Continuing personal and professional development.

Introduction

The first part of this chapter continues our analysis of communication skills by considering NVC. We have already seen that words carry only part of the intended meaning of our message; the remainder is conveyed non-verbally. Thus, NVC usually constitutes a dominant channel of communication for non-factual messages such as conveying feelings and attitudes. We will return to NVC frequently in the following chapters, but here we can analyse its nature and identify some of its positive and negative aspects. The second part of this chapter suggests some principles for effective writing and reading, and analyses how these principles can be applied in practical teaching situations.

NVC

We can divide NVC into three categories: the first is the way we use our voice (paralanguage), the second is the way we use our body (body language) and the third covers proximity and orientation.

Paralanguage

Much of the meaning of what we say is conveyed by the tone, pitch and pace of our voice. The following task from Ellis and McClintock (1994) illustrates this.

PRACTICAL TASK PRACTICAL TASK **PRACTICAL TASK** PRACTICAL TASK **PRACTICAL TASK**

Say *Shut the door*:

- as an order;
- as a question;
- to mean: *shut* that *door, not* this *door;*
- to mean: *shut the door, not the window;*
- to mean: *don't leave the door open as you usually do.*

Note how your voice changes as you change your intended meaning.

Paralanguage also includes filler words such as *OK*, *um* and *eh,* as well as coughs and laughter, and is a major vehicle for conveying attitudes and emotions. We can illustrate this by taking any simple bland phrase, such as *The sun is shining today*, and saying it aloud to convey different emotions (such as happiness, anger and fear) and attitudes (such as lack of interest, smugness or contempt). Try doing this and note how your voice changes as you change your emotion/attitude.

Body language

Our bodies give away far more information than we realise. In fact, you could say that bodies don't talk: they shout. Body language includes facial expression, gestures and posture. It's difficult to decide which of these three is the most important in teaching, but facial expression must be a strong contender.

Facial expression

> The face is rich in communicative potential. It is the primary site for communication of emotional states, it reflects interpersonal attitudes; it provides nonverbal feedback on the comments of others; and some scholars say it is the primary source of information next to human speech.
>
> (Knapp and Hall, 1992, p262)

PRACTICAL TASK PRACTICAL TASK **PRACTICAL TASK** PRACTICAL TASK **PRACTICAL TASK**

Look again at the illustration above on conveying attitudes and emotions. Try repeating the phrase as you watch yourself in a mirror. Note the changes in your expression as your emotion/attitude changes.

Two features of facial expression are particularly relevant to us as teachers and it would be difficult to overstate their importance. These are eye contact and smiling; both have an important place in any teacher's non-verbal repertoire. If you are feeling brave, make eye contact with someone you pass regularly and smile. The chances are that you will receive a smile back. We appear to respond instinctively when people smile at us and it invariably makes us feel good.

Gestures and posture

Shrugging our shoulders and using our hands to make a point are two examples of gestures. One gesture important in teaching is nodding appropriately when learners speak to us. It indicates that we value what they are saying and encourages them to continue. Holding your hands out in front of you with palms up or turned in slightly as if you are gathering up is an embracing message; you are including the learners.

Our body posture – the way we move, stand or sit – tells other people how we feel. Standing up straight indicates confidence and openness, slouching conveys sadness, worry or lack of confidence. If you find yourself in the position of entering a classroom for the first time to teach a group of learners who have the reputation of being difficult, a confident body posture will at least give you a good chance of starting off on the right foot.

Proximity and orientation: the importance of room arrangement

Proximity is the distance we keep between ourselves and others, orientation is our position in relation to others. These elements of NVC are closely related to how furniture is arranged in a teaching room. To illustrate, consider the following task.

PRACTICAL TASK PRACTICAL TASK **PRACTICAL TASK** PRACTICAL TASK **PRACTICAL TASK**

Which of the following seating positions do you think is most suitable for an informal interview or tutorial and why?

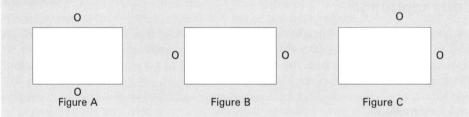

Figure A   Figure B   Figure C

A and B are more formal than C, as there is a physical barrier that separates the participants as they face each other. The greater distance between the participants in B could indicate a higher level of formality, such as that needed for a disciplinary interview. The closeness of the participants in C, plus the orientation of being at right angles to each other, reduces this level of formality and potential adversity. It is the most suitable for an informal interview or tutorial conveying a sense of co-operation and support (Knapp and Hall, 1992).

You may remember an occasion when you went out for a meal with a group of friends, say eight or ten of you, and you found yourself seated at a long table. You could talk to the friends seated on either side of you and to those opposite but it was almost impossible to have any sort of conversation with your friends seated at the ends of the table unless you craned your neck, leaning in front of or behind your neighbour.

REFLECTIVE TASK

Consider how you would you arrange the furniture to facilitate eye contact for a group of about eight learners.

The basics for effective communication are simple: to see and to hear, and to be seen and to be heard. King Arthur probably had the right idea; a round table is a symbol of equality but it also has the advantage that everyone seated can interact easily with each other.

The relationship of group size to who usually speaks in a group is another important factor when considering seating. In a small group of up to about six people, everyone is likely to contribute. Between seven and ten, most people will speak; between about eleven and thirty, a few people (between three and six) will dominate (Rogers, 2007).

One seating problem you probably encounter is learners who become attached to a particular seat that they then see as theirs. For many of us, once we have occupied a certain seat we own it, it's our territory and it makes us feel safe. If we sat in that seat before the coffee break, we return to it afterwards, and if another person is occupying it when we return, we feel put out. So once a learner claims their place in class, they can be reluctant to sit elsewhere. This can make interaction difficult: learners get into the habit of communicating only with those nearest to them. I usually ask everyone to sit in a different place after a break. I have never had a problem with this and very soon the communication flows easily as each learner owns the whole room rather than one seat.

If you are interacting with learners who are standing, you might face a similar situation. In a demonstration, for example, some learners will always stand at the back. Try asking them to move forward and ask others to go back. And if you become aware that a learner cannot see or hear, saying *Come forward if you can't see or hear* might not be enough. You may need to address the learner by name, ask them to come forward and find a place where they *can* see and hear.

Then, of course, your teaching environment may not be a classroom at all. It may be a swimming pool if you are a swimming instructor, a hangar if you are teaching aircraft technicians, a field if you are teaching an agricultural student to drive a tractor, or a hospital ward if you are a nurse tutor. But the principle remains the same: ensure your learners can see and hear you so that they can be actively involved in learning.

Negative NVC

All of us have our own particular style of NVC, our personal gestures and expressions that are peculiar to us. Generally, our learners view these with kindly amusement and, on the whole, it's probably not a good idea to change something that is so much a part of who we are. But some NVC can be irritating and, worse, may convey negative messages to learners.

CASE STUDY

He's not really interested in us
Karl has been attending classes in electrical engineering for about six weeks. Here he is talking about Max, his teacher.

He's pretty OK really, but when he's speaking he walks around the room looking at things or out of the window rather than at us. He certainly knows his stuff though. You can ask him anything and he'll always give you a good answer, but it's like he's the only one who can possibly know anything and every time he says something important, which is quite often, he does this chopping thing with his hand. It's quite funny really; some of the others have this competition to see who can guess when he's going to do it so you get synchronised chopping. He hasn't noticed – yet.

The chances are that Max is blissfully unaware of his unfortunate NVC. But let's just hear what it is saying to Karl (and to the others in the class).

I quite like Max really. I think he's a nice enough guy but I'm not so sure he likes us all that much. Perhaps not like *is a bit strong. I don't think he is all that interested in us. He doesn't make me feel that he'd be really pleased if I did well.*

There are two problems with NVC. The first is that we are often unaware of our own expressions and gestures, especially if they are negative. The second is that our own particular version of NVC does become a habit. So we do need to think about the messages it might be sending to learners and to try to avoid the following:

- Hand gestures such as chopping; they can appear aggressive.
- Folding your arms or crossing them in front of you (as in a self-hug); these are defensive gestures and could indicate that you want to separate yourself from learners.
- Using barriers such as the desk to separate yourself from learners.
- Looking ahead or looking or down at your paperwork rather than at learners.
- Slouching, as it can be interpreted as weariness or lack of confidence.

Using NVC positively

We can send positive as well as negative messages to learners via our NVC. Indeed, I would say NVC is probably one of the most undervalued and underused of our teaching tools. Yet, used correctly, it can motivate learners, increase their self-confidence and self-esteem and make their experience of learning more enjoyable and more successful. We will return to these issues in the following chapters. For now, here are some things to include in your NVC repertoire.

- Make eye contact with every learner to show that you are interested in them.
- Smile; this doesn't mean turning into a Cheshire cat, but smiling shows learners that you are relaxed and that you enjoy being with them. It also encourages them to contribute.
- Nod to indicate agreement when learners contribute; this shows that you are listening and that you value what they say.
- Stand up tall and look at everyone to show you are in charge, and move about the room to show that you want to engage with them.
- Vary the pace and tone of your voice to maintain interest and to emphasise important points.
- Try to gauge the effect of your words on your learners. Focus on their NVC. What are they feeling? Are they interested (sitting up or leaning forward, focusing on you)? Are they worried, bored, confused, or do they disagree (looking around, fidgeting, frowning)?

Writing and reading

When you think about your written communication with learners, it's probably going to be in the form of handouts, presentation aids (such as PowerPoint slides) and feedback. Our role as readers is mainly concerned with reading learners' assignments, essays, reports and so on, so that their progress and attainment can be assessed. This section gives some general advice on reading and writing and then illustrates the points of good practice with reference to situations that you are likely to experience.

General guidelines for writing and reading

One of the anxieties that teachers, especially newly qualified teachers, can experience is to do with their own writing skills. They worry that they will make spelling or grammatical errors.

It is true that your literacy skills need to be good enough to enable you to teach your subject effectively. The requirement of the minimum core is that your skills should be at level two, but you don't need to be an expert in literacy. If you are worried about your writing, there are books that can help. You might want to start with *The Minimum Core for Language and Literacy: knowledge, understanding and personal skills* (Appleyard and Appleyard, 2009). It has chapters on writing, reading, grammar, punctuation and spelling. It also has references to other books if you want to go further.

Here are some points to bear in mind when you are writing for your learners or reading their work. The guidance is given in the context of your own writing but is also applicable to your learners' written work.

Writing should be appropriate for the audience
- Use vocabulary that is appropriate for your readers.
- Always explain technical terms.
- Be wary of using colloquial language and avoid jargon.
- Bear in mind learners with special needs.

Writing should be well organised
- Know what you want to say before you commit it to paper.
- Make a plan.
- Structure your writing in a logical sequence.
- Each paragraph should serve to make a key point in this logical sequence.
- Each sentence of a paragraph should illustrate the key point of the paragraph.

Writing should be clear and concise
- Use straightforward phrasing, for example *It is . . .* rather than *It would seem to be the case that. . .*
- Use a clear font like Times New Roman; ensure it is large enough to be easily read.
- If you are writing by hand, make sure it is clear enough for learners to read.
- Avoid tautology, for instance *please re-write this again*.
- Use diagrams and illustrations where appropriate: charts, spiders and mind-maps are particularly useful for getting a lot of information across and tend to be more appealing than text.
- Use headings and bullet points instead of sentences when appropriate, for example on handouts and PowerPoint slides.

Writing should be correct
- Be sure your spelling, punctuation and grammar are correct.
- Use spell-check but don't rely on it.
- Read through your written work carefully. If you don't, learners will take delight in pointing out any errors when they appear in large letters on a screen or interactive whiteboard.
- Make sure that the content is accurate.

Writing should be consistent
- Use the same textual features such as language, style and format throughout.

- Use the same terms throughout. For example, if you use the term *assignment* don't later refer to the same thing as a *project*.

Let us see how these guidelines can be applied in some practical situations.

Designing and writing display material

One of the most common writing tasks associated with teaching is the design and preparation of material that you use to back up your presentations, usually in the form of PowerPoint slides, whiteboard writing or OHP transparencies. In addition to the general guidelines given above, there are some specific points to bear in mind. We can identify these by looking at a sample PowerPoint slide.

PRACTICAL TASK PRACTICAL TASK **PRACTICAL TASK** PRACTICAL TASK **PRACTICAL TASK**

Look at the PowerPoint slide reproduced below and comment on any way you think it could be improved. Compare your answer with the comments given below the slide.

Grammar: Parts of speech
Nouns
Nouns are the names of things, people, places, thoughts or feelings. There are four types of nouns: common nouns, proper nouns, abstract nouns and collective nouns.
Common nouns name:

objects:	*table, handout, car;*
places:	*town, street, college;*
living creatures:	*frog, learner, women.*

Proper nouns require capital initial letters and are the actual names of:

people:	*Rafael, George, Miriam;*
places:	*Germany, High Street, The Cotswolds;*
organisations:	*McDonald's, Nike, Greenpeace.*

There are several ways that this slide could have been improved.

- The slide is over-crowded, and the teacher has attempted to give too much information on one slide. As this is clearly part of a series, it would have been better to transfer at least half, and possibly more, of the information to another slide.
- The lettering is too small and may be difficult to read from the back of the room.
- Some of the fonts are not clear. The introductory sentences look pretty but are difficult to read.
- This slide suffers from over-complication, exemplified by the use of three different fonts.

In summary, here are some points to bear in mind when designing and writing presentation material.

- Use at least 14pt font and a clear typeface.
- Use short active sentences and avoid jargon. A good general rule is to follow the *KISS* principle, an acronym credited to Kelly Johnson, a Lockheed engineer, and expanded as *Keep It Simple, Stupid!*
- Identify the learning point and use the slide to state it clearly.
- Make your layout attractive. Use headings and bullet points where appropriate.
- Use diagrams and illustrations where appropriate.
- Make sure that your PowerPoint slides are of high quality, look professional and are free of errors. All written material given to learners reflects your own standards of presentation, and high-quality display material puts you in a strong position to demand similar standards from your learners.

Designing and writing handouts

Handouts come in many forms, including information sheets, assignment briefings, worksheets and gapped handouts. The one thing they have in common is that they are all designed and written by a teacher and read by learners. All the guidelines for effective writing apply in equal measure to handouts, and the points listed above concerning presentation slides are also relevant. So what additional guidance is appropriate? Read the following practical task to see if you can identify any further points to take into account when designing and writing handouts.

PRACTICAL TASK PRACTICAL TASK **PRACTICAL TASK** PRACTICAL TASK **PRACTICAL TASK**

Here is a gapped handout intended for learners starting a BTEC National Business Studies course, whose first assignment involves a presentation on marketing. The handout is given to learners to consolidate their understanding of designing PowerPoint (ppt) slides, a topic covered in the briefing to the assignment. What are the strengths and weaknesses of this handout? Note your conclusions and compare with the comments below.

EFFECTIVE POWERPOINT SLIDES

1. Which of the following fonts would be appropriate for your ppt slides on Marketing? Why?
   - Arial
   - Braggadocio
   - Georgia italic
   - Lucida handwriting
   - Times New Roman

2. What would be the smallest appropriate font for your ppt slides?
   - 8pt
   - 10pt
   - 12pt
   - 14pt

3. List 3 ways in which you can alter the letters on your ppt slides to add emphasis.

4. Should you write words in upper case letters on your ppt slides? Why/why not?

5. Should you write words in italics on your ppt slides? Why/why not?

6. Which of the following colours is appropriate for emphasis on your ppt slides?
   - Dark blue
   - Red
   - Yellow
   - Grey

7. How can you prevent the audience looking at a section of one of your ppt slides that you wish them to see later on?

8. List 2 advantages and 2 disadvantages of using sound effects on your ppt slides.

9. The maximum number of words (14pt font) that should be used on one ppt slide is approximately _____ words.

10. List 3 ways in which you could maximise the impact of your ppt slides on your audience and gain their attention.

Overall, this handout meets most of the criteria for effective writing. One of its strengths is that it is interactive; learning will be more effective if the reader has to do something in addition to merely reading the material, and this handout clearly requires a response from the learners. It is also, in the main, consistent, correct, clear and written in language that is appropriate for a group of BTEC National learners.

This is not to say that it can't be improved. Consider the following points.

- This is meant to be a gapped handout where the learners fill in the gaps. However, the questions require a variety of responses, from giving short answers and selecting from a multiple choice.
- There is not enough room on the handout for learners to write all of their answers. One basic rule for gapped handouts is that you should leave sufficient space for learners to add their own comments and annotations.
- Although the teacher may well have given clear instructions on what the learners should do to complete the handout and what they should do subsequently, there is always the likelihood that they will forget. So it is always useful to include administrative detail, such as learner's name, how to complete the task, and what to do after completion.

In summary, handouts should be written with the learners in mind and follow the conventions of good writing. It's worth reiterating that all written material given to learners should reflect your own standards of presentation. If they see that you take a lot of care with your handouts and worksheets, there is less chance that learners will use them as the raw material for a paper aeroplane factory!

Reading learners' work

This section concentrates on the reading techniques that you might use in your communication with your learners. Primarily this concerns reading your learners' work in order to assess their learning, but also reading to prepare your lessons.

The first point to make is that there are several reading techniques at your disposal, depending on the particular task in hand. Let's look at each in turn.

Scanning

This means looking at a text for key words when you are searching for specific information and to see if it is relevant to your task. Reading an introduction or index also comes into the scanning category. This is an appropriate technique when you are in the initial stages of researching a topic you are going to teach.

Skimming

Skim reading involves moving your eyes quickly over headings, titles and text to identify the main points, to determine whether the text is relevant to your needs and to see if you want to read it in detail. This is also an appropriate technique for lesson preparation and for initial assessment of learners' work.

Detailed or active reading

This is about understanding clearly what has been written, when you become involved with the text and take time to read every word to make sure you understand its meaning. This is the appropriate approach for reading texts that are essential for your teaching and for reading learners' assignments.

Critical reading

Critical reading involves evaluating the text and taking a view about its qualities. You will use this technique most frequently when assessing your learners' written work. To do this effectively, you will need the following information.

- What are the criteria for success? What needs to be achieved for a pass, credit or distinction?
- What is the grading system? Is it percentage grading, letter grading or just pass/fail?
- What weighting is to be given for each criterion? For example, if one element is omitted, can excellent work in other elements still gain a pass?

These questions clearly concern assessment rather than reading technique, but be aware that without this knowledge your reading may be compromised. Assuming that you have this information, you are then in a position to begin critical reading of your learners' work, and this needs to be done systematically. One approach, originally developed as reading tips and strategies for graduate students, is known as SQ3R (Robinson, 1970). This stands for *survey, question, read, recite* and *review*, and can easily be adapted to suit your purpose in reading your learners' work. In brief, *survey* equates to skim reading the text to gain an overview and *question* means identifying things in the text that require clarification. The text is then *read* again to elicit answers to these questions and these answers are then *recited*, or noted. Finally, the *review* stage is when you make a judgement on the text in the light of how effectively your questions have been answered.

PRACTICAL TASK PRACTICAL TASK **PRACTICAL TASK** PRACTICAL TASK **PRACTICAL TASK**

Use the SQ3R approach when reading a selection of your learners' written work. Evaluate the advantages and limitations of this approach.

Feedback

Once you have read and assessed your learners' work, you will need to give them feedback. To do this effectively is an art in itself. The key point is to identify the response you wish to elicit from the learner and to estimate the effect your comments will have.

This section comes with a health warning. Organisations have vastly different policies on feedback, varying from not allowing teachers to write any comment on learners' work to giving teachers complete freedom on how they give feedback. In consequence, you need to find out what the policy is in your organisation and to abide by it.

Let's illustrate the main points of giving effective written feedback by looking at Shamim's reaction to feedback she has received on her assignment on assessment.

CASE STUDY
Shamim's assignment
Shamim is a trainee on a CTLLS course. She has just received written feedback from Phil, her tutor, on an assignment where she was required to evaluate three assessment methods that she had used in her teaching practice. She is not happy. Read Phil's comments and see what you think.

Shamim

You have covered the advantages and limitations of essays and multiple-choice questions as assessment methods, but the section on the third method – case studies – is rather sparse, and could have been considered in more detail.

You have shown a good understanding of a range of theories of assessment, and the way you relate Rowntree's writing on the principles of assessment to your experience (page 2 of your assignment) is particularly convincing. This is a good example of linking theory to practise which can serve as a model for future assignments.

You have not included much comment on differentiation. Gemmas assignment does this very well, and you might care to have a look at how she has tackled this.

Your referencing is accurate and comprehensive. However, please note that some of your sentences are cumbersome and you need to write in a shorter, simpler style. There are also one or two spelling and punctuation errors that I have annotated in the margins.

Overall, you have done enough to gain a Pass mark, and your use of theory to justify your opinions and to inform your practice is a strength of the assignment. However, you should note the following action points for future assignments:
* *Make sure you cover all aspects of the brief equally comprehensively. In this assignment, case studies and differentiation were only superficially covered.*
* *Write in short simpler sentences.*
* *Check spelling and punctuation.*

Phil

PRACTICAL TASK PRACTICAL TASK **PRACTICAL TASK** PRACTICAL TASK **PRACTICAL TASK**

To what extent do you feel that this feedback is well written? Note your response and compare with the following comments.

I think the main points that arise from Phil's comments are as follows.

* This feedback is appropriate for a CTLLS trainee. The language is not over-technical and avoids jargon.
* The feedback seems well organised and follows a logical sequence. Phil is clearly following a marking guide that requires him to comment on specific criteria and identify action points.
* On the whole the writing is clear, but not totally concise. Phrases such as *You might care to have a look at* and *Please note that* are wordy and could have been omitted. On the other hand, the action points are a good example of concise writing.
* The feedback contains both a spelling and punctuation error. (I'm sure you will have spotted them, but the answers are on page 44, just in case you haven't.) This is not very impressive when you are criticising such errors in the work you are assessing!

So it seems as though the comments do meet the criteria to a large extent. So why is Shamim unhappy? Let's continue with the story.

CASE STUDY
Shamim's assignment (continued)
Shamim decided to share her feelings about the assignment feedback with her friend Neema.

I worked ever so hard on this assignment, and feel really let down. I can't argue with anything Phil has written: I did make a few spelling mistakes and I was a bit brief on case studies. But I genuinely feel that all his praise is very grudging, and he was just trying to find fault. And I do resent being compared to Gemma, who I don't get on with anyway. As for writing cumbersome sentences, I don't know what he means. Which sentences is he on about? He hasn't marked any of them so I can't work out which he means. So I'm beginning to wonder whether it's worth putting all this effort in. It might be better to judge what I need to do just to get a Pass and do that but no more.

There is obviously more to writing good feedback than just meeting general guidelines for good writing, as Phil's comments have had a de-motivating effect on Shamim, which I am sure is not what he intended. It should be possible to define some general guidelines to writing good feedback so that the learner knows how well they have done and has received precise and supportive advice on what to do in the future. The effect on the learner should be to recognise their achievement, accept their shortcomings and be keen to do better next time.

PRACTICAL TASK PRACTICAL TASK **PRACTICAL TASK** PRACTICAL TASK **PRACTICAL TASK**

How do you think Phil's feedback could be improved, so that Shamim could value what she has done well, and be positive about doing better in future? List your recommendations and compare with the comments below.

Tummons (2007, p71) gives some good advice on constructing effective feedback, which I think is appropriate to this case study. The main points he makes include:

- beginning the feedback by stating the specific strengths of the assignment, and finishing by stressing the progress that has been made;
- being specific in identifying what needs to be developed and stating clearly what the learner needs to do to improve. Race (2005) uses the apt term *feed-forward* to describe the aspects of feedback that focus on what the learner needs to do next;
- assessing solely against the assessment criteria and avoiding comparison of one learner's work with another's;
- including specific action points that the learner can act upon.

If you apply these guidelines to Phil's feedback, it's clear that it could have been written to give more emphasis to the strengths of Shamim's assignment. Also, he could have avoided personal comparisons and been more precise and positive about the shortcomings of the assignment. In this way, Shamim might have felt more positive about the feedback on her work.

A SUMMARY OF **KEY POINTS**

> Become aware of your NVC. Try to avoid using negative gestures; instead, focus on using NVC positively.

> Your written communication, including presentation aids and handouts, should be at an appropriate level for your learners, and be clear, well-organised and correct.

> Handouts and display material should reflect your own high standards of writing and serve as an example to which your learners can aspire.

> Reading learners' work needs to be done systematically, objectively and in the context of the relevant assessment criteria.

> Written feedback to learners needs to be objective and should specifically identify strengths, weaknesses and action points for future development.

Branching options

The following tasks are designed to help you to be more aware of NVC and to consolidate and develop your practical communication skills of reading and writing.

Reflection

Look carefully at the body language of your learners at the start of a lesson and note your observations. Consider how these conclusions might affect the delivery of your future lessons.

Analysis

Examine the handouts you are currently using for your teaching. To what extent do they meet the criteria for good writing and preparation of written aids that are detailed in this chapter? Identify any improvements that could be made and amend the handouts accordingly.

Research

Use the library or internet to research communications skills audits. What do you feel are your strengths and development needs with regard to the communications skills reviewed in this chapter and Chapter 3? Check your conclusions by completing one of the audits you have found. If you have difficulty in finding an audit appropriate to your needs, you may be interested in trying the audit in Appleyard and Appleyard (2009) or in Machin (2009).

Errors in Phil's feedback in case study, page 42

1. Practise is spelt incorrectly. The correct spelling of the word in this context, when it is used as a noun, is *practice*.

2. The phrase *Gemmas assignment* needs an apostrophe in the word *Gemma's,* indicating possession, *the assignment of Gemma.*

REFERENCES AND FURTHER READING

Appleyard, N and Appleyard, K (2009) *The Minimum Core for Language and Literacy: knowledge, understanding and personal skills.* Exeter: Learning Matters.

Ellis, R and McClintock, A (1994) *If you take my meaning: theory and practice in human communication.* London: Edward Arnold.

Knapp, M L and Hall, J A (1992) *Nonverbal communication in human interaction.* Orlando, Florida: Harcourt Brace Jovanovich.

Machin, L (2009) *The Minimum Core for Language and Literacy: Audit and Test.* Exeter: Learning Matters.

Minton, D (2005) *Teaching Skills in Further and Adult Education.* London: Thomson Learning.

Race, P (2005) *Making learning happen.* London: Sage Publications.

Rogers, J (2007) *Adults learning.* Maidenhead: Open University Press/McGraw-Hill.

Robinson, F P (1970) *Effective study* (4th edn). New York: Harper & Row.

Tummons, J (2007) *Assessing learning in the lifelong learning sector.* Exeter: Learning Matters.

5
The human factor in communication

This chapter will help you to:

● recognise the emotional element in your interactions;
● use communication skills to engage with learners and to show empathy;
● use communication skills to help learners build self-esteem.

Links to LLUK professional standards for QTLS:

AS4, AS7, AK4.1, AK4.2, AP4.1, AP4.2, AK5.1, AK5.2, AP5.1, AP5.2, BS2, BS3, BK1.2, BP1.2, BK3.1, BK3.3, BK3.4, BP3.1, BP3.3, BP3.4.

Links to CTLLS:

Unit 2 Planning and enabling learning.

Links to DTLLS:

Unit 2 Planning and enabling learning;

Unit 4 Theories and principles for planning and enabling learning;

Unit 5 Continuing personal and professional development;

Unit 6 Curriculum development for inclusive practice;

Unit 7 Wider professional practice.

Introduction

Looking at the guidelines in the previous two chapters you might be forgiven for thinking that all you have to do to be an expert communicator is to follow the rules for effective speaking, listening, reading and writing. However, things aren't that simple. If we were dealing with computers, rather than people, it might be possible to programme an effective communicator in this way, but we *are* dealing with people, and people have a habit of not always behaving logically and rationally. It isn't just a case of recognising that everyone, on occasion, communicates emotionally as well as rationally. We also need to understand why this is so, and then to develop a communication style that takes into account the human factor in communicating. This is what this chapter is about. The first part concerns understanding yourself, how emotions can affect your communication style and how you can use this understanding to communicate with your learners more effectively. The second part of the chapter focuses on learners, and explores ways to use communication to support them.

Recognising our emotions

We *are* human, with human emotions, which are evident in all of our interactions. Indeed, it is impossible *not to* communicate emotions; they appear in every smile, raised eyebrow, hand gesture and so on. Emotions are vital for teaching. If we had no emotional involvement with learners it would mean we were indifferent to them. They would certainly have great difficulty in relating to us; you can't relate to a robot. It is tempting, though, to cover emotions with the cloak of professionalism: *I never let my feelings get in the way of my job.* This just isn't possible.

The part played by emotion in communication has been well recognised. Salovey and Mayer, for example, define emotional intelligence as:

> ...the ability to monitor one's own and others' feelings and emotions, to discriminate among them and to use this information to guide one's own thinking and actions.
>
> (Salovey and Mayer, 1990, p189)

Childs and Pardey (2005) suggest that it is important to try to understand how our emotions can affect our communication.

> A conscious and focused awareness of both our own and others' emotions plays a critical role in how we manage ourselves as well as how we communicate with others. Emotions shape our reactions to events and to people.
>
> (Childs and Pardey, 2005, p19)

So, how do we set about this task? One place we can look for insight is philosophy. Ancient philosophy, in particular, is full of everyday metaphors that help to explain the rational and emotional elements in our behaviour. In *The Dhammapada* (*The path to wisdom*), attributed to Buddha, you will find an elephant metaphor to represent our emotions and a trainer to represent our rational mind. Plato used the metaphor of a charioteer controlling powerful horses. You will also find the wild horse in the Hindu script *The Upanishads.* I like the elephant best; it is a strong metaphor so it is easy to bring to mind when you need to. It's also easy to remember; I have used it with communication students and they always seem to remember it well, even years later. In ancient philosophy, where there was often a strong emphasis on self-improvement, the goal was for individuals to use reason to identify and manage (or train) their elephant.

How does the elephant metaphor work in practice to explain our behaviour? In his exploration of philosophy and modern science, psychologist Jonathan Haidt (2006) tells us that our elephant behaviour goes back to our primitive responses to our environment – our fight or flight responses. When faced with danger, we needed to make very quick decisions on whether to feel angry enough to fight, or frightened enough to run away. These decisions were instinctive and automatic; there wouldn't have been time to stop and think. Although we no longer face wild animals, we still carry our fight or flight responses, for example, feeling nervous before an important interview. There are occasions in teaching where we might communicate with our emotional elephant in control, for example, communicating our feelings of irritation and frustration to learners who appear lazy and apathetic. These feelings can get in the way of effective communication, so it is in our interests to recognise and manage our own brand of elephant behaviour.

The key to recognising our elephant behaviour lies in understanding our feelings, especially those connected to our fight/flight responses; anger, which also includes feeling irritated, frustrated or annoyed, and fear, which also includes feeling worried or nervous. Let's look at these feelings as experienced by some teachers and expressed in their communication with their learners.

Communication and anger

CASE STUDY

Vince's elephant

One of Vince's plastering learners is describing what it's like to have him as a tutor.

Vince is a great teacher. He is really enthusiastic about us being professional and doing an excellent job and he wants us to be enthusiastic too. This is great for me as I think I'm just as keen as he is. The only thing is...well, it's difficult to explain, so I'll give you an example. Yesterday we were doing some decorative stuff, and Jack's work was really pretty rough. Vince just looked at the work, looked straight at Jack and said, This is just about typical. Your problem is you don't think.

REFLECTIVE TASK

Why do you think Vince spoke to Jack the way he did?

Vince's enthusiasm for his subject, and his ability to convey this enthusiasm to his learners, is to be applauded. But he is angry because he feels that Jack can't be bothered to do a reasonable job and his anger has influenced how he communicates. It has leaked out as a judgement about Jack, and a *put-down*. Vince hasn't recognised his feeling of anger, nor what has triggered it, in time to stop an emotional outburst.

Vince's anger was conveyed to Jack through his choice of words as well as his NVC. But it is our NVC that usually carries most of the emotional content of our message. This is illustrated in the following case study.

CASE STUDY

Sue's elephant

Sue is ten minutes into her session when the door opens and Kiera slips into a seat at the back. Sue waits until Kiera is seated, then slowly looks around at everyone in the class and sighs as she drawls, *I see Kiera's on time again this morning*.

PRACTICAL TASK PRACTICAL TASK PRACTICAL TASK PRACTICAL TASK PRACTICAL TASK

What emotion do you think Sue is expressing? How is it expressed? Note your response and compare with the following.

Sue is feeling irritated because, yet again, Kiera hasn't managed to get to her class on time. Sue's irritation has leaked out as sarcasm. Sue's message to Kiera is delivered non-verbally; the way she looks around the room, the sigh and the change in the tone of her voice to a drawl. Sue hasn't recognised her feeling of irritation, nor what has triggered it, in time to moderate her response.

In fact, two messages are being conveyed here and they are contradictory, which is how sarcasm works. The phrase *I see Kiera's on time again this morning* doesn't, in itself, carry a critical message. Kiera could be a good timekeeper and Sue could be praising her time-keeping to the rest of the class, but we know this isn't the case because of Sue's NVC. Sarcasm usually makes people feel uncomfortable and it can be confusing if our words pass one message but our NVC something different.

Communication and fear

Fear can also affect the way we communicate. There are some fears that are specific to teaching and can affect just about every new teacher. During my research for this book, 30 DTLLS trainees told me about their fears. The overwhelming majority of trainees had experienced fear about:

- looking foolish;
- failure;
- not being able to manage the learners.

Let's look at two teachers to illustrate how fear and anxiety can influence our communication with learners.

CASE STUDY
Fay's elephant

Fay has a problem with her attitude to one of the learners in her Creative Writing course, and here she writes about it in her journal.

I taught the second session of the Creative Writing course today, and was mortified to discover that Richard, who turned up at the last minute, has had a couple of books published. When he introduced himself, he dropped all these names of publishers, agents and writers that he had met, and I began to wonder if he should be teaching the class rather than me.

But the problem really started when Mercedes read out the piece she had written about her childhood in Spain. It wasn't very well written, but it was clear that she had worked hard on preparing it, and it was very creditable for someone writing in a foreign language. Anyway, when I asked for comments, Richard immediately jumped in with some very critical remarks that clearly impressed the rest of the group, and before long I felt he was taking over the class.

The thing is, I didn't feel confident enough to confront him, which I know I should have done. To tell the truth, I was afraid that he would show me up because he appeared to have more experience than me, and it was easier to let him carry on. Stupid really – I know very well what I should have done, but somehow my anxiety got the better of me.

Fay's behaviour is dominated by her fear of challenging Richard; her elephant is at work. It is stopping her voicing her honest feelings about the way Richard is dominating the class. Most of us can recognise this situation; we fail to do something even though we know what we should do, because we are frightened. We know that Fay really wanted to intervene because she admits her fear in her journal. Now that she has recognised her fear and why she felt frightened, this could help her to challenge Richard more effectively in future.

CASE STUDY
Paula's elephant

Paula is an accountancy lecturer who is under stress. At the moment she has just finished an AAT (Association of Accounting Technicians) class where her mind is on other things. In particular she is late for a meeting with her external examiner and is worried about a couple of her learners who are likely to fail the course.

This worry has affected her communication with Kit, one of her most conscientious learners, as shown by this conversation Kit has later with his friend Tipu.

Kit: *I'm fed up with my course. I don't feel I'm getting anywhere and I wish I could just leave.*
Tipu: *Why, what's happened?*
Kit: *Well, this afternoon I didn't really know what I was supposed to be doing and I really needed to get this presentation sorted out.*
Tipu: *Well, why didn't you ask for help?*
Kit: *I did ask but Paula said it would have to wait. She said she would email me pronto to fix something up, but that's no good to me. I need to get this sorted now because it's my turn to do the presentation at work next Monday.*
Tipu: *Well you should have made that clear to Paula.*
Kit, getting irritated: *I did try and explain but she said she was already late for a meeting. She was packing up her stuff in a hurry and she seemed preoccupied. The department secretary had also come in and was badgering her. I don't think my problems even registered, which shows how important I am in her order of priorities!*
Tipu: *Let me buy you a beer.*

PRACTICAL TASK   PRACTICAL TASK   PRACTICAL TASK   PRACTICAL TASK   PRACTICAL TASK

What is Paula frightened of and how has her fear affected her communication with Kit? Note your response and compare with the comments below.

Paula has allowed her worry about the forthcoming meeting to control this interaction. She is frightened that she'll be late for the meeting, so she tells Kit she'll email him and they can arrange to meet up. There does appear to be time for Kit's problems to be sorted before his presentation at work but Kit isn't happy. So what is really bothering him?

The answer is found in Kit's final comment, *I don't think my problems even registered, which shows how important I am in her order of priorities.* Kit is fed up because he feels that he isn't important to Paula. It's not Paula's verbal message, but her NVC, that is telling him that she isn't really interested and that perhaps she doesn't even care. This is unlikely to be true, although it is true for Kit because this is the message that he has received. Paula hasn't recognised how her feelings of anxiety have affected her communication with one of her learners.

Managing our emotions

Not all elephant behaviour is bad; some of our best actions are emotional and spontaneous, but the elephant can be a barrier in our interactions with learners. The important thing to remember is that we all have feelings and that we are responsible for them; we all have an elephant and we own our own elephant. No one else can make us feel angry or worried, only ourselves.

Recognising and managing the emotion in our communication doesn't come easily. It involves reflection, together with commitment. Reflection itself can be uncomfortable and it is especially so when emotions are involved. If we add to this the subtlety and complexity of the communication process, it soon becomes clear that it is something that needs to be worked at. Abraham Maslow recognised the difficulties involved.

> *Self-knowledge and self-improvement are very difficult for most people. It usually needs great courage.*
>
> (Maslow, 1998, p180)

The best way to manage the elephant is to treat it with kindly affection and gently train it. We don't want to lock it up and throw away the key; we just want to make it behave so that it doesn't jump out unexpectedly. It is possible to manage your feelings or, in the terms of this metaphor, to train your elephant when you are communicating with learners. Here are a couple of suggestions.

- Look for the emotional element in all your interactions. Learn to recognise how your particular elephant behaves. Does it make excuses? Is it reluctant to pass messages or to challenge, choosing instead to avoid conflict at all costs? Or does it interrupt when others are speaking, speak loudly or dominate the conversation? Does it make judgements, use sarcasm or put-downs?
- Learn to recognise the feelings that bring the elephant out in the first place. Do you feel anxious, uncomfortable or scared? Do you feel irritated, frustrated or downright angry?

The guidelines given in Chapters 3 and 4 for effective communication, particularly those concerning speaking, listening and NVC, are important tools for training your elephant. Thus, if you have trained your elephant you:

- are confident in expressing thoughts, feelings and wishes;
- are aware of the effect of your verbal and non-verbal messages on the listener;
- are relaxed and speak with a confident, clear voice;
- don't drag up the past or make comparisons;
- don't make veiled hints;
- don't judge others;
- don't blame others or try to make them feel guilty;
- don't use sarcasm or *put-downs*.

There is another reason why we need to look inwards, to be aware of and to manage our emotions. Put simply, if we don't understand ourselves, how can we possibly understand our learners?

> *...the more open we are to our own emotions, the more skilled we will be in reading [others'] feelings...*
>
> (Goleman, 1996, p96)

Recognising learners' emotions

We have been looking at the influence of emotions in our communicative interactions with learners, so you won't be too surprised to read that learners also have emotional elephants. It is part of our professional role to communicate with our learners in a way that recognises their emotions, that is sensitive to them but also taps into them to encourage learners to feel confident and valued.

There are some key skills here that are fundamental to our communication. First, there is the ability to engage with learners, to show that we like them and want them to be successful and to enjoy their learning. Second, there is empathy, the skill of being able to imagine what it must be like to be the learner, as opposed to the teacher. Third, there is the ability to react to learners' emotions in order to increase their levels of confidence and self-esteem. It is difficult to separate these strands, but let us start by looking at the contrasting communication styles of two teachers, operating in similar situations, that require the ability to engage and to empathise.

Engagement and empathy

CASE STUDY
Rick and Cara

A Tai Chi course has been advertised at the leisure centre. The response has been phenomenal so it has been decided to divide the class into two. Rick and Cara, the Tai Chi instructors, are to work in adjacent studios. It is the start of the first session and Rick and Cara are ready to begin work.

In studio one Cara finds a group of about 25 people waiting. She introduces herself, *Hi, I'm Cara and I am your Tai Chi instructor*. She then asks everyone to take a seat along one side of the studio and she pulls up a chair to face them. She tells the group that she needs to give them some background information (what to wear, registration and so on) before they begin. The information takes about 20 minutes to get through and Cara is keen to begin, so she briskly says, *Now, does anyone have any questions before we get started?* There is no response so Cara gets to work. She is a good instructor, carefully showing her learners how to do the different movements until they feel confident that they've got it. At the coffee break Cara suggests that everyone gets a drink from the machine and brings it back to the studio. She then goes to a desk in the corner and starts on her paperwork. The learners, meanwhile, have seated themselves in a line along the wall. One or two have introduced themselves and are chatting; others are sitting alone.

In the adjacent studio Rick greets his group. He looks around at everyone, smiles and says he is really pleased to be there. He tells everyone to grab a chair and gather round as he has some things he needs to tell them. He begins by speaking briefly about his own love of Tai Chi. Then there is quite a lot of enrolment information to get through, so he decides to spend only ten minutes on it and leave the rest until after the coffee break. After ten minutes is up, he smiles at the learners and says that he is sure they must have lots of questions which he will do his best to answer. One of the learners says that she is worried she won't be able to remember the different movements. At this, Rick nods his head in encouragement and three or four others agree it's something they too are worried about. There are a few relieved giggles as people agree that they will look a bit silly if they turn one way and everyone else turns the other. Rick is able to calm their fears, telling them that this worry is normal, that yes, it happens to just about everyone at one point or another. Then they put the chairs back and get to work. Rick is a good instructor and soon it is the coffee break. While everyone goes out to get their drinks Rick quickly moves the chairs back into a rough circle. As people return with their drinks and sit down, Rick checks that he has everyone's name correctly and makes sure that they all have someone to talk to. Once everyone has had a chance to chat, he asks whether they have any questions about the moves they have covered. By now everyone feels pretty relaxed and a number of people make comments and ask questions. They finish off the coffee break feeding back to the class one or two things they have discovered about their fellow learners during their chat. As they begin work for the second part of the session Rick realises that they have gone well over the coffee break time but he thinks it is time well spent.

PRACTICAL TASK PRACTICAL TASK **PRACTICAL TASK** PRACTICAL TASK **PRACTICAL TASK**

We know that both Rick and Cara are good Tai Chi instructors. If you were thinking of attending a Tai Chi class would you prefer to be in Rick's class or Cara's class? Why? Note your response and compare with the following comments.

I know whose class I would prefer to be in; Rick's, and the reason is because he was able to engage with his learners and to put himself in their place, to imagine what it must be like to be them. Cara, on the other hand, missed many opportunities to do this. Let's look at her missed opportunities.

- At the start of the session Cara gave the learners all the information on the course in one go. In itself, this is fine, but it meant she felt pressed for time and a consequence was that she was fairly brisk when she asked the learners if they had any questions. They are likely to have sensed her desire to begin work from her choice of words, *Now, does anyone have any questions before we get started?* Clues were also to be found in her NVC (we know she spoke briskly, and she may already have begun to gather up her paperwork). None of this would have encouraged anyone to voice their worries.
- At the coffee break Cara physically separated herself from the learners by going to the corner of the studio and doing her paperwork.
- At the coffee break Cara left the seating as it was (in a line along the wall). This arrangement didn't encourage the learners to get to know each other and Cara wasn't aware that some learners were sitting alone. Perhaps you think this wasn't really Cara's responsibility, that the learners should take the initiative. In fact, they often do, but not always.
- Cara didn't give the learners an opportunity to tell her how they felt about the first half of the session.
- Cara didn't give the learners a chance to say anything about themselves.

You might feel that it isn't necessary or appropriate to communicate with learners in the way that Rick did in order to teach them effectively, but communication in teaching isn't really just about being friendly, it's about supporting learners in a very practical way. Rick's learners felt able to voice their worries because they knew from the way he communicated with them that he really understood what they were experiencing.

We don't know why Cara didn't engage or empathise with her learners but I think it is worth speculating on one possible reason. She might have been concerned about being too friendly. This concern is often connected to a very understandable fear of not being able to manage (or control) learners unless you keep some distance. In fact, in some situations it *is* more appropriate for the teacher to keep some distance. To illustrate this, let's go back to the coffee break. Cara left the learners to sort themselves out on their own, whereas Rick spent his coffee break with them. This is a choice we all have to make if we are involved in delivering teaching sessions where a coffee break is included.

The question of staying, or not staying, in the coffee break, in many ways sets the scene for the ongoing relationship between teacher and learners. Some learners will benefit if you are available to talk and listen to them in an informal setting, many will see it as an opportunity to raise issues they would be unlikely to raise in class sessions. On the other hand, others will see your joining them for the break as an intrusion; you should certainly make a smart exit if the conversation stops the moment you sit down. As a general rule though, the closer your experience is to that of your learners, for example if you and your learners have a similar age, background and interests, the more likely it is that they will gain from a more informal relationship with you. On the other hand, if there is a big age gap between you and your learners, with the consequent likely scenario of different interests and backgrounds, an informal relationship is less appealing. In any event, the important thing is to be focused on your learners, to be able to put yourself in their place and be sensitive to their needs.

Let's now see if we can draw out some general points from Cara and Rick to illustrate the practical skills of engaging and empathising with learners.

- Show learners that you like them and enjoy being with them. Rick showed that he enjoyed the company of his learners by smiling, telling them a little about himself, encouraging them to ask questions and arranging the furniture in a relaxed circle.
- Show learners that you think they are important and take their needs into account, for example, being aware that a learner is sitting alone and might feel isolated. Rick made sure that everyone had someone to talk to.
- Try to imagine being the learner. Rick was aware that some of his learners were anxious and he encouraged them to air their anxieties by the way he posed his question, *I'm sure you must have lots of questions,* and by his supportive NVC.
- Learn and remember every learner's name. This is probably one of the most valuable things you can do to facilitate a relaxed and welcoming environment. Name games can be incorporated into ice-breaking activities. The best ones are those that are fun, as laughter draws people together. The most important part of any name game is that every time a learner addresses another they must use their name. If they forget (which they always do, to everyone else's amusement) they must go back and start again, which means names get repeated. It is just as important to address learners by name in ongoing interactions with them. Don't go overboard. *Good morning, Jim, Good morning, Jo, Good morning, Fred, etc.,* is likely to be met by bemusement and amusement; just get into a name-using habit rather than a name-forgetting habit.

Self-esteem

Let's look now at communicating to increase learners' self-esteem. We saw in Chapter 2 that self-esteem is our sense of our own worth, the value we place on ourselves. In his hierarchy of human needs model, Abraham Maslow (1970) recognised the importance of self-esteem to our well-being. Maslow identified two esteem needs: we need to believe in ourselves and we need recognition from others. We all have a craving for the approval of other people, we all need to believe we are important and we all need to feel valued. When any one of us experiences failure or humiliation, it really damages our self-esteem.

Psychologist Denis Lawrence's work on self-esteem and literacy suggests that people with low self-esteem sometimes feel angry, for example they might appear boastful or arrogant, or blame others to boost their self-confidence. Alternatively, they might withdraw, for example, be reluctant to answer questions or be anxious about participating. Let's look at one learner's experience to illustrate this.

CASE STUDY
I want to crawl away

Sam is studying GCE A level History. Along with half a dozen other learners, she is about to begin a discussion on the major social changes of the early part of the nineteenth century. So far, Sam has been enjoying the course and has felt pretty OK about how she is doing. But all this is about to change as the teacher says to her, *Sam, would you record your group's discussion points as I don't think you've had a turn yet*. As everyone in the group turns expectantly towards her, one of Sam's anxieties rears its ugly head. The fact is, she is far from confident in her spelling and grammar skills. As yet, there's not been a problem as she has always checked her written work carefully before handing it in. But she can't do this now. She must write the key points of the discussion. If she makes an error, everyone will notice. She can't refuse because the others will ask why.

During the discussion period, Sam is so consumed with worry that she is unable to make any verbal contribution. At the end of the discussion, when it is time for Sam to feed back her written key points to the class, her friend Jess picks up Sam's sheet containing the points and says, *I'll read these out if you like Sam*, and begins to read through the list: *1 The rise of the Labour party; 2 The introduction of a social welfare system; 3 The emaciation of women.*

This last point is met by howls of laughter from everyone in the class. Sam pretends to see the funny side and laughs along with everyone else, but inside she's definitely not laughing. Jess passes the list back to Sam, saying, *I think you'd better read the rest of these,* so Sam continues with the list of key points. It's difficult for her to speak but she manages to struggle through.

PRACTICAL TASK PRACTICAL TASK PRACTICAL TASK PRACTICAL TASK PRACTICAL TASK

How do you think Sam is feeling as she reads out the remainder of the list? How might her feelings be apparent to the teacher? Is there any way the teacher could have prevented this situation? Note your response and compare with the comments below.

The chances are that Sam feels embarrassed and foolish. She won't have failed to interpret the laughter from the other learners as a sign of her failure, even though it is unlikely this is how it was intended. Her literacy mishap has become public property because communication skills are almost always visible for everyone to see and judge. Her self-esteem is likely to be damaged and it might take a while before she regains her former confidence levels.

If Sam's teacher had been observing her when he asked her to record the group's discussion points, he would have realised she was anxious. It would have been evident in the expression of dismay on her face. If he had been observing her as she read out the remainder of the key points he couldn't have missed the clues, her drooped shoulders and expressionless voice. He would also have noticed that Sam was quiet for the rest of the lesson.

Sam's teacher obviously didn't know that asking her to record the group's work would cause her such a problem. Perhaps he should have, but that's another story. He was aware, though, that she hadn't so far volunteered for this job, and this alone should have alerted him to a possible problem. But even at the stage of asking her and observing her response, there was still an opportunity for him to change his mind and ask someone else.

It is very easy to lower a learner's self-esteem. There are some obvious things that are guaranteed to do this, such as using sarcasm and put-downs, but just forgetting the basics can have the same effect. This is how you do it.

- Forget to praise a learner.
- Forget to encourage a learner.
- Forget to ask a learner what they think.
- Forget to use a learner's name.
- Forget to show any interest in learners.

If Sam's self-esteem plummeted, Jess's probably increased as she made the class roar with laughter when she read out Sam's error. And this is the other side of the coin. When we receive praise (or applause, as in Jess's case), it boosts our self-esteem. Hopefully, most of our learners will have healthy levels of self-esteem, but here's the funny thing: no matter how much self-esteem we have, we always feel good when it's bolstered. It's as if we can't have too much of it. Nor can learners.

Here are some suggestions for ensuring learners have healthy levels of self-esteem.

- Be aware of your learners' NVC. Does anyone look uncomfortable, puzzled, angry or worried? Listen to their voice. Does it carry the same message as their words or is there another message? Observe their expression and their body posture. Is there something they want to say? Their NVC will surely convey the very messages that they find difficult to articulate.
- Be aware of situations that might make a learner feel anxious. Bear in mind the learner who lives in fear that you will put them on the spot or the learner who is embarrassed by their poor grammar or spelling.
- Praise small successes, effort or improvement.
- Show you are interested in what learners have to say, their ideas, viewpoints, enthusiasms and so on.

PRACTICAL TASK PRACTICAL TASK **PRACTICAL TASK** PRACTICAL TASK **PRACTICAL TASK**

In your next teaching session, look for opportunities for boosting the self-esteem of your learners.

A SUMMARY OF **KEY POINTS**

> **Some of our emotions can be a barrier to communicating, so it is important for us to recognise our communication style and the effect it might have on learners.**

> **Show learners that you enjoy being with them and that they are important.**

> Try to put yourself in the place of your learners, to anticipate their needs and to allay their anxieties.

> It is easy to lower self-esteem when you fail to show interest or put learners in situations that expose their weaknesses.

> You can help learners to build self-esteem when you address them by name, praise their successes and are interested in their ideas and views.

Branching options

The following tasks are designed to consolidate and develop your understanding of the role of emotion in interpersonal communication.

Reflection

Consider your recent teaching to identify occasions when you think you communicated with your learners particularly well or particularly badly. To what extent did feelings of anger or fear affect the quality of these interactions?

Analysis

Think back to a lesson when you met a group of learners who were attending your class for the first time. What signs of anxiety did they display? How did you try to allay these feelings? Note the aspects of your approach that were successful or that did not work. Identify any changes you would make to your communication strategy in future.

Research

In this chapter we have considered the concept of emotional intelligence, with reference to the work of Daniel Goleman. Use the internet and the library to research this further, within the context of how the concept is reflected in interpersonal communication style.

REFERENCES AND FURTHER READING

Childs, J and Pardey, D (2005) *Mindchange: the power of emotionally intelligent leadership.* Cirencester: Management Books 2000 Ltd.

Goleman, D (1996) *Emotional Intelligence: why it can matter more than IQ.* London: Bloomsbury.

Haidt, J (2006) *The Happiness Hypothesis: putting ancient wisdom and philosophy to the test of modern science.* London: William Heinemann.

Lawrence, D (2000) *Building self-esteem with adult learners.* London: Paul Chapman Publishing.

Maslow, A (1970) *Motivation and personality.* New York: Harper.

Maslow, A (1998) *Towards a psychology of being.* New York: John Wiley & Son.

6
Communicating for inclusivity

This chapter will help you to:

- be more aware of preconceptions and value judgements;
- communicate with learners to promote equality and respect for diversity;
- communicate with learners to promote inclusivity.

Links to LLUK professional standards for QTLS:

AS3, AS4, AS7, AK3.1, AP3.1, AK4.1, AK4.2, AP4.1, AP4.2, AK5.1, AP5.1, BS1, BS2, BS3, BK1.2, BP1.2, BK2.2, BP2.2, BK3.1, BK3.2, BK3.3, BK3.4, BP3.1, BP3.2, BP3.3, BP3.4.

Links to CTLLS:

Unit 1 Preparing to teach in the lifelong learning sector;

Unit 2 Planning and enabling learning.

Links to DTLLS:

Unit 1 Preparing to teach in the lifelong learning sector;

Unit 2 Planning and enabling learning;

Unit 4 Theories and principles for planning and enabling learning;

Unit 5 Continuing personal and professional development;

Unit 6 Curriculum development for inclusive practice;

Unit 7 Wider professional practice.

Introduction

The theme of inclusivity runs throughout the LLUK standards and other LLUK documents such as *Inclusive Learning Approaches for Literacy, Language, Numeracy and ICT* (the supporting guide to the minimum core, November, 2007). Communicating for inclusivity, ensuring that all learners are involved and no learner feels isolated, is also a concept that is fundamental to this book. In this chapter, we will explore how some related themes are reflected in the communication process. In the first part we will see how preconceptions and value judgements have the potential to exclude. In the second part we will see how the recognition of diversity and promotion of equality and inclusivity can be applied in a practical teaching situation.

Preconceptions and value judgements

Suppose I were to ask you whether you make value judgements about others. My guess is you might say something like, *I don't think I do.* Alternatively, you might just skate over the question, as I have often done with this type of question that seems to require an obvious negative response. But, of course, you *do* make value judgements, as I do, as we all do, and on the whole we do it unconsciously. Let's try this out by considering this adaptation of an old riddle.

A man and his teenage son went climbing. The son fell and sustained serious injury. He was rushed to hospital and taken straight into theatre. However, the surgeon recognised the boy and said, *I can't operate on him, he is my son*. How could this be?

How long did it take you to find the answer? Two seconds? Five? Twenty-five? Unless you knew instantly that the surgeon was the boy's mother, you will have made a value judgement about who a surgeon is; a man but not a woman.

We saw in Chapter 2 that we are constantly involved in a process of receiving and interpreting information about others as we negotiate our way around our complex social world. Our evaluation of other people is often immediate and we are pretty skilled at doing it. We can weigh up another person within seconds of meeting them. Indeed, we often weigh up others before we meet them, on the basis of what we have heard about them, as you might have done with the riddle.

Think about reading through a list of names of prospective learners. Would the name *June* on a list make you think of an older learner, or would the family name *Saville-Wyer* conjure up an image of someone wealthy? In many ways, gleaning what we can about our learners beforehand helps us to plan how we can best support them. When we meet them we pick up signs from what learners are wearing, from their expression, from their body posture, their gestures and the sound of their voice. We interpret these in the light of our expectations, our experience and within the context of the interaction to form an impression of what sort of person they are.

I remember one particular value judgement I made about a learner very early on in my teaching career. From the information I had received about her prior to the start of the programme (she was educated to a high level with a PhD in theology), and from the initial interview (she was articulate and knowledgeable), I labelled her as someone who would enjoy taking on an active role in class discussion. I couldn't have been more wrong. During the first session I confidently asked her to sum up the conclusions her group had reached following their discussion. I can still recall the look of horror on her face. I had assumed that she would be very confident in speaking when, in reality, she was far from confident. Indeed, she was extremely shy, only managing one-to-one situations with some effort. Nor had I noticed that she had contributed almost nothing to the group discussion. As an inexperienced teacher, I hadn't yet quite got the hang of observing what went on in every group. I learnt a powerful lesson from this learner about the potential danger of making value judgements.

Sometimes we interpret information we receive from others to form a generalised or stereotypical picture of them. You can make a stereotype out of any group of people. You can use their physical characteristics (short, blond), their job (police officer, tax inspector), their interests (golfer, plane spotter) and so on.

PRACTICAL TASK PRACTICAL TASK **PRACTICAL TASK** PRACTICAL TASK **PRACTICAL TASK**

You can try this task on your own but it is better with a friend. One of you suggests a category, *all politicians*, and the other responds immediately, *talk rubbish*. You might be surprised at your unconscious assumptions. Here are a couple of categories to get you started: *all teenagers, all Southerners, all bikers*.

There are two problems with labelling and stereotyping learners. The first is that, once in place, labels can be hard to shift; we can hang on to our views regardless of whether or not they are accurate. The second problem is that it can set in motion a communicative chain reaction that results in the label or stereotype becoming reality, referred to as a *self-fulfilling prophecy* (Hargreaves et al, 1975). This is how it works. Our view of someone influences how we interact with them. We have expectations *of* them that we then communicate *to* them. They, in turn, pick up our expectations and adjust their response accordingly, thus fulfilling the prophecy. If, for example, we believe that a learner isn't too interested in the subject because they choose to sit at the back and are reluctant to make eye contact, we might have low expectations of them. We then convey our low expectations to them, perhaps by involving them less than other learners, and they, in turn, begin to lose interest.

> ### CASE STUDY
> **Anything to oblige**
> Amy is talking about the teachers on her psychology course.
>
> *They are both really nice and make the classes interesting but they are very different. One of my teachers thinks I could do really well with a bit of effort. She writes encouraging notes on my work, which is nice, so I always check my written work carefully before handing it in. My other teacher really praises you when you come up with something original so I always make sure I'm paying attention in his classes. I think he likes us to think on the spot.*

One of Amy's teachers may see her as conscientious. She communicates this view to Amy who then adjusts her behaviour (checking her written work). Amy's other teacher may well see her as someone who can think on the spot. He communicates this view to Amy who then adjusts her behaviour (paying attention).

The preconceptions we may have about learners and the value judgements we make about them have the potential to exclude. For example, a prospective learner turns up with body piercings and tattoos and, unless we have a class full of learners with body piercings and tattoos, we may already expect them to behave differently from the other learners. We can't discard our preconceptions at the drop of a hat. What we can do is examine our interactions with our learners and try to identify where we might make value judgements.

Equality and diversity

In developing an inclusive approach to the way we communicate with learners, the QTLS standards emphasise the importance of promoting equality alongside diversity.

> *AP2.2 Teachers in the lifelong learning sector … develop their own practice in promoting equality and inclusive learning and engaging with diversity.*
>
> (LLUK, 2006, p3)

Let's begin by defining diversity and equality. We'll take diversity first. Thompson suggests that it embraces both our human uniqueness and the social groups that each of us belongs to.

> *Diversity relates to the fact that we are all unique individuals [and] to the fact that society is made up of various groups to which power, influence and opportunities are unequally allocated.*
>
> (Thompson, 2009, p92)

We could define equality as treating everyone the same, but with this definition equality and diversity appear to be mutually exclusive. If equality means treating all our learners the same, how can this fit in with diversity, which means respecting and responding to individual differences? The solution to this paradox lies in thinking more deeply about what we mean by equality. Wallace offers us two ways to understand it.

> *We could answer that equality is about fairness and even-handedness; that it requires us, as teachers, to ensure that we show no favouritism or antipathy... [or] our focus is not on what we do (show no favouritism, treat them equally, and so on) but on what we believe... So, we now have two ways of understanding what we mean by equality. It can be about how we act towards our learners, or it can be about how we value our learners.*
>
> (Wallace, 2007, p46)

Wallace goes on to say that when the focus is shifted from what we *do* (show no favouritism, etc.), to what we *believe* (that we should value *all* learners equally), this shift in focus also directs our interactions; in other words, equality of approach is a natural consequence of equal value. I came across a good example of how a teacher gives equal value to learners when talking to Veronica, a CTLLS trainee who is just starting her teaching career as a lecturer in Spanish. She described her feelings about her learners. *I was very excited – I was thinking about how I could make the learners a group, they were all so different. I felt so proud of them and of me and I felt privileged.* There is no doubt that with this approach Veronica will have no conflict between promoting equality alongside diversity. Now we need to consider how we can apply the concepts of inclusivity, equality and diversity in our communication with our learners.

Communicating to promote inclusivity, equality and diversity in practice

Perhaps the best way of illustrating how communication can reflect an inclusive approach, that takes account of equality and diversity, is through a case study.

CASE STUDY
Finn's English literature class

Finn teaches English literature in an adult education centre near Bristol. He is keen to treat his learners equally, to recognise their differences and to ensure that none of them feels left out. Nine very different people have enrolled for his next course. He is reading through the information he has about each of them and wondering how he might communicate so that everyone feels welcome and part of the class. Here is the information that Finn has collected from his learners following an informal chat with each of them.

- John and Joyce have just retired and have decided that they are not going to let their minds go to seed. John worked for a number of years in heavy industry and as a result is partially deaf. He has recently had a knee operation that has resulted in him being wheel-chair bound, albeit temporarily.

- Stephan and Mari are from Poland and speak English reasonably well. They have been in the UK for four years and are now UK citizens. They have considerable knowledge of Polish literature and became interested in English literature following the course they attended for the citizenship test.
- Mishal wants to do something for herself after many years where her children's needs came first. She is thinking ahead about a possible career but, as yet, has no idea what. The English literature course is a first step to getting some qualifications. She has not been in education since her schooldays.
- Ghulum and his girlfriend Vickie thought it might be fun to try out a class and English literature is the only one they could agree on. Ghulum prefers to bring his laptop to classes as he lives with dyslexia and Vickie is wondering how the rest of the class will react to her strong Northern accent.
- Hai Ling is from China. She taught English in Shanghai for over ten years and has always loved English literature. Her English is excellent and she is now studying part-time for a Master's degree to develop her career. She sees the English literature class as time for herself.
- Curtis has been made redundant from his job as a production manager in the motor industry. His daughter has nagged him to do something else apart from answering job ads and filling in application forms. He's not too sure about this class as his memories of school are fairly negative.

PRACTICAL TASK PRACTICAL TASK PRACTICAL TASK PRACTICAL TASK PRACTICAL TASK

How might you advise Finn to ensure his approach recognises his learners' differences but is inclusive and promotes equality? Which of his learners would Finn particularly need to bear in mind when communicating and what should he do? Note your response and compare with the comments below.

Let's have a look at the issue of equality first. If Finn intends to communicate with his learners on an equal basis he will probably be thinking about speaking to each learner in the same way, devoting the same amount of time to talk to each and so on. If, however, he is going to value each learner equally, it is really about his feelings towards them rather than going through the motions. So how Finn feels about his learners is going to influence just about all his interactions with them, from not making value judgements to being aware that some learners will be anxious, to showing his interest in every learner, to being enthusiastic and so on. And, like Veronica, Finn can even begin to feel excited about what each learner can bring to the group and to feel pride in what they can achieve together.

The second part of the practical task, where you had to decide which learners Finn would need to bear in mind, was a bit of a trick question because, of course, every one of these learners will require Finn to adapt his communication in some way. So, in practical terms, what would Finn actually need to do? Well, there are a number of points that he might want to think about. He might want to consider:

- the culturally diverse nature of his group and how each learner understands language;
- how some language could exclude one or more of the learners;
- specific difficulties that some of his learners might have;
- the anxieties that some of his learners might have.

Let's take these points in turn and see what Finn's learners have to say.

Language and culture

Some of Finn's learners are from cultures where the rules and conventions that govern communication may be very different from what Finn is used to. Hai Ling, particularly, is from a culture that places far greater emphasis on politeness.

In China it is not part of our culture to talk to strangers, and especially foreigners, so it can be difficult for Chinese people here to speak in class. It can sometimes look as though a Chinese person doesn't know the answer when, in fact, they know very well. (Hai Ling)

So Finn needing to be sensitive to the cultural differences of his learners, in this case would understand why Hai Ling might be reluctant to speak in class.

He can also use these differences positively for the benefit of the whole group. All of his learners will have knowledge and skills as a result of their individual experience or culture. This knowledge can provide a valuable resource for Finn, and he can encourage his learners to share knowledge and experiences from their own culture with the rest of the group.

Stephan and I love Polish literature and it is going to be really interesting for us to compare Polish and English writers. (Mari)

Here is a great opportunity for Finn to get Stephan and Mari to talk about their interest in Polish literature.

There is one more thing that Finn might want to think about. He has three learners for whom English is their second language. Yet this group in itself is diverse. While Stephan and Mari's English is adequate, Hai Ling's is excellent. She is well educated and is currently studying for a Master's degree. So Finn needs to keep an open mind and not make any general assumptions about learners from other cultures.

REFLECTIVE TASK

Think about your own learners. Do you have learners from different cultures? If so, can you identify diversity within this group?

Language that excludes

Language can be exclusive in different ways. One example is the language we use to describe specific difficulties, such as Ghulum's dyslexia.

I get really irritated when people refer to me as dyslexic. If someone has a limp you don't refer to them as a limper, just someone with a limp. I'm no different. I'm just a guy who happens to have dyslexia. (Ghulum)

Male-dominated language can exclude. We are all so used to male-dominated language that its exclusivity doesn't usually register. In fact, we are more likely to notice attempts to change it, for example *women and men*, rather than the more usual *men and women*. Even so, it is certainly good practice for inclusivity to use gender-free language, for example, *police officer* rather than *policeman*.

Culturally specific language can also exclude. We already know from Chapter 2 that the meaning of any word depends on individual interpretation based on experience, context and so on. This means that the way we understand language is, to some extent, influenced by place and by culture. So learners for whom English is a second language might struggle to understand language that is culturally specific. It also means that even learners such as Ghulum and Vickie, who are from a different area of the UK, could have a different under-standing of some words.

Vickie and I are from the north of England and it's funny how they have so many words and phrases down here that we don't recognise. For example, they say It's getting dimpsey, *meaning it's getting dark, and* blethering, *meaning complaining.* (Ghulum)

Inclusive learning approaches for literacy, language, numeracy and ICT (LLUK, November 2007) gives a number of examples of good practice when communicating with ESOL lear-ners. All the examples they give are good practice with all learners and I have already covered a number of them in Chapter 3. Here are the remainder.

- Use visual clues, titles and intonation (stress on certain words in a sentence, rise and fall of voice) to indicate the key points.
- Pre-teach key words, terms and phrases which may be unfamiliar to the learner.
- Consider the context to decide if it might be culturally dependent and provide appropriate explanation.
- Be aware of terms that have different meanings in different contexts.
- Avoid or explain culturally specific material.
- Recognise that politeness strategies vary culturally. Learners may be confused by instructions that are too mitigated, for example, *I wonder if you might try . . .* as opposed to *Try . . .*
- Recognise cultural differences in non-verbal communication and be sensitive to any miscommunication.

Specific difficulties

Some learners will have specific difficulties. They might, for example, be partially sighted, have learning difficulties or be a wheelchair user. John' and Ghulum's situations illustrates this.

I wear a hearing aid but it has limited use because it amplifies everything. This is bad news when there is a lot of background noise. I have some hearing and I'm pretty good at lip reading as a sort of backup to the words I miss, but I have to be able to see the speaker's face to do this and not everyone is accommodating. It's not their fault, they don't do it on purpose, but you'd be surprised at the number of people who mumble their words, look away or look down when they speak to you, or speak with their hands in front of their mouth.

All this is made worse at present because I'm stuck in this dreaded wheelchair. I never realised how awkward, helpless and frustrated this would make me feel. As well as the obvious things like negotiating steps and narrow entrances, I hate being looked down on, literally, by people who are standing up. (John)

To deal with John's hearing problem, Finn would need to speak clearly and make sure John could see his face, ensure there is good lighting and a quiet environment and to find out from John what he actually needs. The wheelchair issue raises points about access, seating arrangements and a sensitivity to John's frustration at being so restricted. It would be a good idea, for example, for Finn to make sure that he sat down to talk to John so that they were literally at the same level.

I have my own strategies to manage my dyslexia. For example, one problem I have is with memory but I'm quite good at using mnemonics. I also manage most things OK as I have a laptop that goes everywhere with me. (Ghulum)

Finn would need to talk to Ghulum to find out what his needs are, as well as check that Ghulum has understood him and has had time to record important points on his laptop.

The *Access for All* document (DfES, 2001) states that at least eight and a half million people meet the Disability Discrimination Act definition of disability. It offers some useful guidance for supporting learners with a range of learning difficulties and disabilities.

Learners' anxieties

We saw earlier that some learners will be anxious and Finn's group is no exception. We already know that our anxieties can affect the way we communicate. Jenny Rogers explores learners' anxieties in *Adults Learning* (2007). She suggests that two anxieties predominate; looking foolish and being exposed to failure. A prime candidate with the potential to make learners look foolish and expose them to failure is poor or uneven literacy/communication skills.

Many learners, especially those for whom English is a second or third language, or those with specific learning difficulties such as dyslexia, will be anxious about their literacy skills, especially undertaking any piece of writing. Other learners, who may be very knowledgeable about their subject, will have struggled for years with spelling and grammar. Indeed, most learners are likely to have an uneven or spiky literacy profile; in other words, have one or more aspects of literacy skills with the potential to cause anxiety. There is the graduate, for example, who is very capable of writing a thesis but who has never quite grasped how to use apostrophes. So you could say that most learners probably have some anxiety about their literacy skills.

REFLECTIVE TASK

Think about your own literacy skills. Would you say you are completely confident about writing logically and coherently, using well-constructed sentences with the correct grammar, punctuation and spelling?

Some learners will suffer secret agonies about one or other of their communication skills. Mishal and Vickie are in this category.

I'm really worried that we will be expected to word process our essays. I'm actually quite frightened of using a computer. (Mishal)

I come over as very confident, but in fact I'm very conscious of my strong Northern accent. Everyone here speaks quite posh. Will they laugh at me? Will they be able to understand me? (Vickie)

These are very real fears. Will they be put on the spot? Will they be expected to know about ICT? Will they be required to speak in front of a group of people or, even worse, a class? ESOL learners in particular and learners with hearing or visual difficulties are likely to be worried. Will they be able to understand the teacher? Will the other people in the class understand them? Will people laugh at them?

Learners also worry about whether they will cope with their learning. Some will have experiences or memories of school that have dented their self-confidence or left them feeling they are not as clever as their fellow learners. There is also a very real fear among many older people that as you age, you are less able to learn. Rogers (2007) provides evidence that this isn't the case, but the idea is so widespread that many older people accept it as a truth. Mishal, Curtis and Joyce have these fears

I haven't studied anything since I was at school. Will I be able to manage? (Mishal)

It really gets to you when you keep filling in application forms and they don't even acknowledge them. You lose confidence in yourself after a while. Will the others on this course ask me what I do? What will I say? (Curtis)

You don't remember as well as you get older and I am worried that everyone will know more than I do. John's not worried and he says I'll be fine and I probably will, but I still have that worry. Will I look stupid? (Joyce)

How Finn communicates with these learners will make a difference to how they manage their anxieties and, of course, it would need to include a plentiful supply of encouragement and praise. You might want to re-read the section in Chapter 5 on building self-esteem.

We have been talking so far about how Finn interacts with his learners, but he will also want to raise awareness within his group of the importance of valuing and respecting all members of his class. Of course, one of the best ways he can do this is by his own example, but he also has a duty to actively promote equality and diversity. This means he will want to encourage his learners to listen to each other without judgement and to treat each other with respect and courtesy, and he will need to step in if a learner makes an inappropriate comment or value judgement. In any event he should be aware and prepared.

In the above case study we have looked at how Finn can value each of his learners through his communication with them. If he is to do this successfully there are two very important practical things he can do. The first is to take the time to get to know his learners, to talk to them and, more importantly, to listen and to keep listening. The second is to get into the habit of observing his learners. If he can become an expert in interpreting their NVC he will know when they are feeling uncomfortable, confused, hesitant or unhappy without them having to say a word.

Here are some general communication strategies for inclusivity.

- Find out as much as you can about your learners beforehand. If possible, try to talk to every potential learner to introduce yourself and to welcome them to the course.
- Ice-breaking activities, especially those that are fun, are always a good way to make learners feel welcome and part of the group.

- Give everyone plenty of opportunity to be successful: one good way to do this is to tap into their individual knowledge, interests and enthusiasms.
- Arrange seating so that everyone can see and be seen.
- Ensure good lighting and try to eliminate background noise.
- Make sure that learners who have missed a session have access to notes.
- Don't make generalisations about learners. Always talk to them to find out what they need.

A SUMMARY OF **KEY POINTS**

> The value judgements we make about learners may influence the way we communicate with them.

> When we stereotype learners we have certain expectations of them. We may then communicate these expectations to them and they, in turn, may adjust their behaviour in response.

> In promoting diversity and equality we need to recognise individuality but treat every learner with the same value and respect.

> Linguistic and cultural differences can make communication more difficult for some learners.

> How we communicate with learners can affect how well they manage their anxieties.

> We need to listen to learners, observe their NVC, show interest in them, give them opportunities for success and praise often.

> Some learners may need individual help, for example use of a keyboard or to sit in a certain place.

Branching options

The following tasks are designed to help you consolidate and develop your understanding of inclusivity and how equality and diversity are reflected in the communication process.

Reflection

Reflect on an occasion when you have pre-judged an individual learner. What was the basis of your initial judgement, and how did this affect your communication with this particular learner? How will this experience affect your future approach to new learners?

Analysis

Review the group of learners that you used for analysis in the branching option of the previous chapter. Analyse how you would promote inclusive learning and ensure that no individual learner within this group felt excluded from the learning process. Note your conclusions in your journal, and review your strategy as the course proceeds.

Research

Wallace gives two different ways of understanding the concept of equality in teaching situations. One way is based on how we behave towards our learners, the other on how we value them. Use the library and the internet to evaluate this concept of equality in more detail, illustrating your conclusions with reference to your own teaching.

REFERENCES AND FURTHER READING

DfES (2001) *Access for all*. London: DfES.

Hargreaves, D, Hester, S K and Mellow, F (1975) *Deviance in Classrooms*. London: Routledge and Keegan Paul.

LLUK (2006) *New overarching professional standards for teachers, tutors and trainers in the lifelong learning sector.* London: LLUK.

LLUK (June 2007) *Addressing literacy, language, numeracy and ICT needs in education and training: defining the minimum core of teachers' knowledge, understanding and personal skills.* London: LLUK.

LLUK (November 2007) *Inclusive learning approaches for literacy, language, numeracy and ICT.* London: LLUK.

Rogers, J (2007) *Adults learning*. Maidenhead: Open University Press/McGraw-Hill.

Thompson, N (2009) *People skills*. Basingstoke: Palgrave Macmillan.

Wallace, S (2007) *Teaching, tutoring and training in the lifelong learning sector*. Exeter: Learning Matters.

Websites

inclusion.uwe.ac.uk
www.odi.gov.uk
inclusion.ngfl.gov.uk
www.qcda.gov.uk

7
Managing behaviour through communication

This chapter will help you to:

- communicate to deter disruptions;
- communicate to manage disruptions.

Links to LLUK professional standards for QTLS:
AS3, AS4, AS7, AK4.1, AK4.2, AP4.1, AP4.2, BS2, BS3, BK1.2, BK1.3, BP1.2, BP1.3, BK2.2, BP2.2, BK3.1, BK3.2, BK3.3, BK3.4, BP3.1, BP3.2, BP3.3, BP3.4, DK2.2, DP2.2.

Links to CTLLS:
Unit 1 Preparing to teach in the lifelong learning sector;
Unit 2 Planning and enabling learning.

Links to DTLLS:
Unit 1 Preparing to teach in the lifelong learning sector;
Unit 2 Planning and enabling learning;
Unit 4 Theories and principles for planning and enabling learning;
Unit 5 Continuing personal and professional development;
Unit 6 Curriculum development for inclusive practice.

Introduction

One of the dominant fears that new teachers have is that some of their learners will disrupt their teaching. Perhaps this is the result of memories of baiting a teacher at school or from reading newspaper reports of teachers being driven to distraction by learners who are out of control. Although the reality is rarely as bad as we may fear, there is also no doubt that we all come across very difficult teaching situations, where disruptive behaviour provides a significant challenge to our attempts to stimulate and manage learning.

The theme of this chapter is that effective communication skills can be a significant factor in deterring and managing disruptions. The first part of the chapter reviews the main elements of communication style that discourage disruptive behaviour; the second part looks at how effective communication can be used to manage some difficult teaching situations.

Effective communication to deter disruptions

I believe that if you communicate effectively with your learners, if you engage with them and establish a rapport based on mutual respect, and if your approach is inclusive and supportive, then disruptions are far less likely to occur. It will not have escaped your notice that all these elements of effective communication style have been covered in the preceding chapters, so we are already well on our way to preventing disruptions. So what can we do over and above this? One valuable tool we have at our disposal is our ability to communicate with confidence; another is communicating with politeness and professionalism. Lastly, there is our own genuineness and our willingness to accept learners for who they are. Let's take these in turn.

Communicating with confidence

If your confidence levels are not as high as you'd like them to be, all is not lost. Race and Pickford (2007) suggest that it isn't necessary to actually *feel* confident, only to be *perceived* as confident by learners, so it's more a case of practising to *look* confident rather than *being* confident, although it has to be said that the more you practise being confident, the more confident you become. Here are some suggestions for signalling confidence.

- Use eye contact and your smile to show your interest in the learners. It would be difficult to overstate the importance of eye contact. When others make eye contact with us we feel included and valued. Eye contact also indicates that you are aware of each and every learner, so be careful to include *all* learners and not just those at the centre/front of the room.
- Own the whole room; move around calmly from learner to learner, standing tall and with an awareness of everyone in the room. This shows that you are in control. Don't speak against noise. Wait until it is quiet and you have everyone's attention. Be confident to wait.
- Be aware of your facial expression. Is it anxious or weighed down? Remember that concentration can also give this appearance. What you are looking for is an open, positive expression, with your head up, as if you are relaxed and about to smile. This shows you want to engage with learners and also conveys your positive expectations of them. Remember the self-fulfilling prophecy; if you convey through your communication, especially your NVC, the expectation that your learners will be enthusiastic and motivated, and that anything less than this is just not on your agenda, the chances are that they will pick up your expectations and adjust their responses.
- Be approachable, welcoming and ready to listen, but also be clear about your expectations of learners.

REFLECTIVE TASK

Identify someone you know who you feel is a confident communicator. What is it about them that gives this impression?

PRACTICAL TASK PRACTICAL TASK PRACTICAL TASK PRACTICAL TASK PRACTICAL TASK

1. Stand in front of a mirror and observe your face. Now alter your expression to convey: (a) enthusiasm and interest; (b) confidence; (c) anxiety.
2. Take a sentence from a book and read it out loud. Now read it to convey enthusiasm and interest. Use the tone of your voice and pauses to emphasise. Go overboard and exaggerate to get the feel of it. Now read the sentence to convey confidence and, finally, anxiety.
3. Repeat this second task looking in a mirror. Notice the change in your expression as you convey the differing emotions.

Politeness and professionalism

In the previous chapter we looked at how easy it is to stereotype learners. When I returned to learning as a mature student, I very quickly became aware that a small minority of people stereotyped me as *a student* and this then influenced how they communicated with me. I remember one particular occasion, in a college library, when the librarian was impolite and brusque to the point of rudeness. It was as if she felt it wasn't necessary to make any effort to be polite and courteous to students. I had previously worked for many years in commerce and remember being taken aback by this new experience. More to the point, it discouraged me from wanting to be polite in return. The point I want to draw from this little anecdote is that we can't expect politeness from learners unless we are polite. Indeed, learners deserve exactly the same levels of politeness and courtesy as any other group of people. Now it isn't always easy to bear this in mind, especially when a learner is disrupting your class, but making a conscious commitment to politeness and courtesy, whatever the situation, is part of our professional role.

Genuineness and acceptance

In *Building self-esteem with adult learners* (2000), psychologist Dennis Lawrence offers some advice that I think you might find helpful for preventing disruption. Lawrence talks about the twin concepts of genuineness and acceptance. Genuineness is really about being yourself, having the self-confidence to be your own person, to say what you believe and feel even if the reaction is disapproval. For example, you may feel that it is inappropriate for a learner to turn up late for your class without giving a reason or apology. You know that this message might be met with disapproval, but you have the confidence to pass it anyway.

The other side of this coin is acceptance. It is inevitable that some learners will have values and opinions that are different from yours. Some of these might be very different. Acceptance means:

> being able to accept the person unconditionally even if you disagree with their views, or even with their behaviour.

(Lawrence, 2000, p42)

This is pretty much what Carl Rogers (1983) called *unconditional positive regard*. It doesn't mean you have to change your views, just accept that others are entitled to their views and feelings. For example, the learner who was late might have felt that there was no need to apologise because they had a good reason for their lateness. Lawrence also stresses the importance of empathy, the ability to convey to learners that you are able to see things from their point of view. So, in this case, showing empathy would mean communicating to the tardy learner that you need to be told why they were late, but that you also appreciate that there was a good reason for their lateness and that you realise that, on occasion, it just isn't possible to be on time. Showing empathy through active listening skills and supportive NVC diffuses potential conflict and helps to build respect and trust, even though, for a small minority of learners, it can take some effort on our part. (You might wish to re-read the section on recognising learners' emotions in Chapter 5.)

One problem with acceptance is that we can't fake it. If someone expresses views that are radically different from ours, for example, extreme political views, we may go through the motions of saying we understand how they feel but the chances are that our true feelings about the issue will leak out through our NVC. So it's more a case of working towards a greater understanding of our own beliefs and values. If we recognise our own beliefs and attitudes we are better equipped to accept others' right to theirs.

Managing disruptions

Teaching is about people interacting with each other – learners with other learners and with us – so it's not possible for every class to run smoothly and easily every time, much as we would like it. Things will happen. Someone rambles on, someone wants to dominate the group, someone gets irritated and so on. Learners are also more vocal in letting teachers know if there is something they don't like. Some learners get bored through no fault of the teacher; they have shorter attention spans and crave constant variety. They hop quickly and easily from *Facebook* to their iPods and expect the same versatility in their studies. Despite our best efforts to prevent problems, there will still be times when learners can be disruptive. And learners are no different from us. When we get irritated or anxious, it shows in our interactions. When learners feel angry, scared, confused and so on, it shows in their inter-actions, even though they may not recognise how they feel, nor necessarily be aware that their behaviour is a problem.

Disruptions come in many forms, from sullenness and hyperactivity to rudeness and aggres-sion. Few of us are natural experts at communicating. It is a skill that requires effort and this is especially so when a situation arises where our emotions are prodded, for example when a learner challenges us or engages in behaviour that we see as unacceptable. It is all too easy to respond with irritation or annoyance.

Let's have a look at some examples of disruptive behaviour and draw out some general conclusions about using communication to manage it.

CASE STUDY
The sullen learner
Alison has just completed her nurse training. Here she is talking about her first experience of education as an adult and how her fear of being shown up affected her interaction with her tutor and with others on the course.

I hadn't been in a classroom since school and found the whole thing pretty uncomfortable. I seem to remember that I thought that everyone else in the class was cleverer than me and they always seemed to know the answers and know what to do. Looking back, I don't know why I found it so hard, but I suspect it had a lot to do with my lack of confidence because I hadn't done any studying. I think I made things difficult for Lizo, our tutor, because I wouldn't volunteer anything and if he asked me a question I would only say the bare minimum.

I know I made things difficult for the others too because I wouldn't join in any of the group work. I think I must have come across as sullen and not interested, when in fact I was in a panic most of the time because I thought I would be shown up as a fraud. So I can understand why some of them were reluctant to work with me. I can't blame them – I didn't want to work with me. They must have thought I was quite aggressive too because if anyone asked me to do anything, I remember I just said No! *I never gave a reason – you can't really say,* No, I'm too scared, *can you?*

PRACTICAL TASK PRACTICAL TASK **PRACTICAL TASK** PRACTICAL TASK **PRACTICAL TASK**

How do you think Lizo might have been able to help this learner? Note your response and compare with the following comments.

The chances are that not one of the learners in this group had any idea that Alison was frightened. They probably thought that she was just naturally miserable. We can see that her sullen and aggressive attitude was a shield for her lack of confidence, so Lizo would have been thinking about ways to increase Alison's confidence.

- He could have found a quiet moment to chat with Alison and ask her if she had any worries. With supportive NVC (eye contact, a smile) and encouragement, the chances are that Alison would have told him about her fears.
- He could have given Alison lots of opportunities to experience success, perhaps by asking her a question that he was confident she could answer and gradually encouraging her to say a little more.
- He could have given Alison lots of praise whenever she made a contribution to a discussion or answered a question. Even if the answer wasn't correct he could have praised her good attempt.

CASE STUDY
The domineering learner

Vicente has just completed a marketing course and he is talking about one of the other learners on the programme.

There was this bloke on the course, Keith. He was one of those people who have a lot to say and he got on everyone's nerves. It didn't matter what we were talking about, he knew all about it. Whenever we were working in a group he would go on and on and, if you didn't watch it, he wouldn't let anyone else have a turn. And if someone did manage to get a few words in he'd jump straight in and interrupt them. No one wanted to work in a pair or group with him. Actually, there was one guy who didn't mind and that's only because he was lazy – he'd just sit back and let this Keith do all the work. It was the same when Bill, the teacher, was doing something with the whole class – Keith just wouldn't shut up. Luckily though, it didn't take Bill long to sort him out.

PRACTICAL TASK PRACTICAL TASK **PRACTICAL TASK** PRACTICAL TASK **PRACTICAL TASK**

Can you suggest any reasons why Keith always wanted to dominate the conversation? If you were Bill how might you have managed to *sort him out*? Note your response and compare with the following.

When a learner won't stop talking and, as in this case, appears rude and aggressive, it can make life very difficult for other learners, to say nothing of the teacher! There are different reasons why learners won't stop talking. Very early on in my teaching career I had a learner who started talking the moment she walked into the room and didn't stop until she left, and I really struggled to manage this problem. I remember organising lots of group work with considerable movement between the groups so that no one had to listen to her for too long. It helped, but wasn't ideal and certainly isn't enough on its own. But I quickly discovered that this learner used words as a shield for her anxiety; when she became anxious she couldn't stop talking. Other learners talk because they feel that they aren't being heard. Yet others have a need to be the centre of attention and occasionally a learner wants to take over the class. Despite these different reasons for learners talking, strategies for managing it are pretty similar. As for *sorting Keith out,* I expect that Bill probably used some of the following tactics that you can try if you are in a similar situation.

- Step in and stop a learner who wants to dominate the discussion. Direct eye contact might be sufficient on its own but, in some cases, you will need to spell out that the learner has spoken at length and it is time for someone else. You can then direct a question at another learner. Be prepared for the talkative learner to come back almost immediately.
- During class discussions, don't allow a talkative learner to interrupt. Again, you have to be pretty clear and decisive in your choice of words and your NVC. Sometimes a talkative learner will wander off the subject and you might need to bring them back. You could ask them to sum up in one sentence.
- When organising group work, everyone needs to be clear about how much any one learner should speak. They might find using a talking stick helpful for a talkative learner or one who constantly interrupts. (A talking stick is an object held by the speaker – if you are not holding the talking stick you are not allowed to talk.)
- You might give the talkative learner an opportunity to speak in a controlled situation. For example, you could ask them to research a particular topic and speak about it for a set time.
- If a learner persists in talking (or indeed, with any unwanted behaviour) you could try going right up to them, making eye contact, addressing them by name and being clear about what is acceptable or, alternatively, taking them aside for a quiet word.

CASE STUDY
The discordant group
Krista teaches sports science and is working towards DTLLS. She has about 25 learners who are working in groups of four or five to complete a joint assignment. When Krista becomes aware of raised voices in one of the groups, she quickly goes over to the group and says sternly, *Stop this noise and get on with your assignment.* One of the learners says, *It's got nothing to do with us, it's those two, they're having a row.* Krista turns to the two involved in the argument; they are both scowling. She glares at them and tells them again, louder this time, they are making too much noise and they are to get on with the work. One of the learners complains, *He swore at me.* Krista ignores this comment and says, *You have only twenty minutes left to get something down on paper so you'd better get on with it.* The group gets on with the task but there are some resentful looks.

PRACTICAL TASK PRACTICAL TASK **PRACTICAL TASK** PRACTICAL TASK **PRACTICAL TASK**

What are your thoughts on how Krista handled the conflict in this group? How do you think her choice of words and her NVC affected individual learners and the group as a whole? What suggestions might you make to Krista about how she could manage this situation? Note your response and compare with the following comments.

Krista began well when she moved over to the group immediately she became aware of discord, but from then on things started to go downhill. Let's look at some of the things that went wrong for Krista.

- Her NVC (stern look, glare, raised voice) would immediately appear to the learners as aggressive. She allowed her irritation to get in the way in this interaction and to influence her communication.
- Her choice of words indicated to the learners that her main concern was that they get on with the task. Now, this does seem a good idea – after all that's what they should be doing – so Krista was right to bring them back to this, but her choice of words, *Stop this noise and get on with your assignment,* conveyed her irritation. Nor did she say anything to the learners to show that she understood how they might be feeling, or that she was remotely interested in what had happened.
- She ignored the NVC of the two learners involved in the argument and didn't listen to the comment made by one of them. This too will have indicated lack of interest in what they had to say and no understanding of how they might feel.
- Her final comment, *You'd better get on with it,* would be seen as a threat. They may knuckle down but this won't have changed what they think or feel.
- She missed an opportunity to talk with the group (or class) about how they want to interact with each other.

We can now look at how Krista might have interacted with the learners. Clearly, her aim was to get the learners back on task. Perhaps it *was* really important for the task to be completed by the end of that session. But if not, Krista can achieve quite a lot in the space of just a few minutes that, in the long run, will benefit everyone.

- She could approach the group calmly and with an open, positive expression (with her irritation elephant well out of the way).
- She could ask the group what the problem was and whether she could help, and use her NVC (eye contact with each member) to support her words.
- She could listen to what both learners involved in the argument had to say. Listening actively, without value judgements, to how they feel helps build trust and paves the way for problem solving. The chances are that this would be enough to defuse this situation, but if not, she could offer to try and help them to sort it out at the end of the class or at a later convenient time.
- She could encourage the learners to focus on the assignment. She could praise them for returning to the task in hand. She could ask how they are getting on and perhaps make some suggestions and use her NVC (eye contact, smiling) to show her appreciation and to indicate her expectation that they would be keen to finish the task.
- If the task could be left to another time, she could use the time for everyone to discuss what they expect in terms of respect and courtesy from each other.

CASE STUDY
The challenging learner
Vasu is an experienced child-care teacher. Here she recalls a situation early on in her teaching career.

I still wince when I think of this incident. We had just been discussing what to do if a baby wouldn't stop crying and I was saying that I wanted them to write down some of the points we had covered. The whole class was involved; it was going well and I was unprepared for what happened next. Completely out of the blue, Briony said, I don't agree with anything you've said – in fact, I think it's total rot and I'm not going to write anything. *I was completely thrown off course; I suddenly felt unsure of my facts. Was I speaking total rot? But I also felt very angry at Briony. She hadn't been the easiest of people to get along with, prickly and sometimes abrupt almost to the point of rudeness. I think all my previous irritations with her surfaced and, to my shame, I blurted out,* Well, if you're not prepared to work I'm not prepared for you to stay. *At this, Briony stood up and said,* Suits me. *And she turned to her friend who also got up. Then they both walked out. The rest of the class just sat in silence and, you know, I could see on their faces that they felt really sorry for me but they also knew I'd messed it up.*

PRACTICAL TASK PRACTICAL TASK **PRACTICAL TASK** PRACTICAL TASK **PRACTICAL TASK**

How do you think Vasu might have responded to Briony to bring about a different outcome? Note your response and compare with the following comments.

Vasu allowed her anger at Briony's rudeness, and her fear that she might have said something that wasn't correct, to get in the way. This is another example of the emotional elephant controlling communication. And she issued an ultimatum to Briony that was just about impossible to reverse.

When this sort of situation arises, one of the pressures on us is being able to make a very quick assessment about what is happening, what we want to happen and how this can best be achieved by what we say next. Do we make a point, do we ignore it, or do we laugh it off and chivvy the learner along? As often happens in teaching, the answer to these questions is *It depends*, and you need to be flexible. It depends on how serious the incident is and how important it is to you that it shouldn't be left. There's no doubt that pretending blissful ignorance and having a sense of humour are hugely useful. But it is unlikely that Vasu would want to do either as this is a direct challenge. So, what could she do?

The best option for Vasu would be to stay calm rather than getting angry, but this was probably easier said than done because Briony's outburst was very much like a personal attack. Vasu certainly took it personally – *I suddenly felt unsure of my facts* – but it wasn't her fault. It's much more likely that Briony's own problems were the catalyst for this outburst and a more sensible option for Vasu would be to attempt to find out, through dialogue, what was behind it. It would help Vasu if she could accept that Briony has the right to feel angry but, obviously, not to be rude.

Let's say that Vasu stays calm. This means thinking about her NVC; no clenched fists, frowns or scowls: instead maintaining eye contact with Briony and an open, positive expression. This gives her a breathing space to decide on the best outcome and how she can achieve it. She could then engage with Briony in a challenging but non-threatening way. Keeping her voice steady and positive, she could ask Briony to explain what she doesn't agree with and actively listen to what she has to say. She may have to persist, as Briony might be reluctant to expand. At the same time, Vasu would need to take note of Briony's NVC as this will give her vital clues to how Briony is really feeling. Vasu can then decide what she wants Briony to do and explain it carefully, using her NVC to indicate that she expects a positive outcome.

Vasu may decide that she is willing to negotiate with Briony to achieve a compromise that they are both happy with. If so, she would need to be clear in her own mind about her own boundaries and what is acceptable to her within a range of possible options, for example, complete the writing, work on it at home, write about a different topic or something else.

There is one more thing to consider before we leave Vasu and Briony. The emphasis in this chapter (and indeed throughout the book) has been on interacting with learners with our negative emotions firmly out of the way. This is because they can disrupt our communication. But this doesn't mean that learners should never be aware that we have feelings; far from it. We work hard to communicate our feelings of enthusiasm for our subject and our learners, and our pleasure when learners are enjoying learning. And there is nothing better than laughing with our learners at something we all find funny. Sometimes, though, we want learners to be aware of our negative emotions, of our anger or our disappointment, and we shouldn't be reluctant to pass these messages. Saying we feel angry is very different from communicating in anger. Disclosing our feelings to learners is just that, passing a message that we feel angry or worried.

There is probably only one rule to bear in mind when passing a negative message about how you feel: separate the person from the action that has catalysed your negative feeling. Vasu communicated to Briony in anger, *Well, if you're not prepared to work, I'm not prepared for you to stay.* Let's say that Vasu decides to disclose her feelings of anger to Briony. During their dialogue she might say to Briony, *You make me feel angry when you are rude.* Although this is better than communicating in anger, it would be even better if Vasu separated Briony from the action that catalysed her anger: *I feel very angry when anyone is rude.* This removes the accusation from Briony, while still passing the message of her feelings of anger. And, after all, this is more honest because we know that no one else can *make* us feel angry or frightened or, indeed, any of the emotions we feel. We own our own elephant: each of us is responsible for our own emotions.

CASE STUDY
The wrecker
Rex is a key skills tutor who is contracted to teach a group of eight long-term unemployed learners on a Return to Work course. Here is an extract from his journal.

I'm dreading next week and having to deal with Gary again. He is 26, never had a job and isn't keen to find one. He's only on this course because he risks losing benefits if he doesn't attend. All he wants to do is to keep drawing dole money, watch daytime TV and win the lottery!

So for the last two weeks he's come to the class on sufferance and, to alleviate his boredom, has decided to bait me and convert the other seven learners to his lifestyle. He gets under my skin by doing tasks like writing CVs and application letters deliberately badly so that I have to spend an inordinate amount of time correcting his work. Then he will take out a cigarette and pretend to light it, while still in the classroom. Worse still, he thinks it's clever to boast to the others about never having had a job and offers to give them tips on how to get more benefits by fiddling the system.

The problem here is that he is very articulate and persuasive. The other learners really do want to get back into work, but having Gary around is a major distraction and his presence tends to wreck everything I'm trying to teach them. What do I do? Do I ignore him or confront him? Help!

PRACTICAL TASK PRACTICAL TASK **PRACTICAL TASK** PRACTICAL TASK **PRACTICAL TASK**

What do you think Rex should do, and how should he communicate this to Gary and the rest of his group? Note your conclusions and compare with the comments below.

There is a world of difference between believing that good communication skills can have an effect on behaviour (the theme of this chapter) and that they can solve all behavioural problems that we are likely to face. Some situations require action that can vary between referring to a college manager, using disciplinary procedures, reporting to employers and so on. This is probably the situation here; even if Rex were an expert at using all the communication skills we have discussed so far, there is no guarantee that Gary's behaviour would change.

This doesn't mean that he should just give up. In addition to coping with Gary, he has to take into account the effect of Gary's disruptive behaviour on the rest of the group. The danger is that by concentrating on dealing with Gary, by reacting to his attention-seeking and challenging actions, the other learners feel ignored. Thus, we get to the unhappy situation where Rex appears to be giving more value to a disruptive learner and excluding those who genuinely want to learn. So the first point to make is that Rex should deal with Gary in a way that does not reward his behaviour at the expense of the other learners.

The choice between confronting and ignoring is probably too crude. One approach would be to talk to Gary away from the group, to make the boundaries of acceptable behaviour clear, and what the consequences would be if he did not abide by them. Another approach would be for Rex to talk to the whole group, reviewing and negotiating his expectations of acceptable behaviour without singling Gary out, but giving him the opportunity to make his point as part of a whole group discussion. As ever, the best solution depends on specific circumstances. The result will, to a significant extent, depend on Rex's communication style in tackling this issue with Gary and the rest of the group.

In conclusion, all the communication skills we covered in Chapters 3 and 4 are even more important in dealing with disruptions. The skills of speaking clearly, listening actively, observing learners' NVC, giving learners opportunities to be successful and offering honest praise for their efforts, all need to be employed. In addition to these skills, here are some general guidelines for managing disruptive behaviour.

- Be clear about expressing to your learners the expectations you have of them.
- Don't allow a learner to dominate discussion, constantly interrupt or talk when another learner is speaking.
- Keep your own emotional elephant well out of the way. Don't get irritated, angry or anxious. The best way to do this is to imagine stepping outside yourself and observing what is happening. This mentally separates you from the problem and helps you to realise that it isn't directed at you personally. Stay calm, be aware of your NVC, be supportive and positive, but clear about your expectations.

A SUMMARY OF **KEY POINTS**

With the proviso that communication skills alone may not resolve all problems of disruption, a communication style that includes the following elements will discourage and minimise disruptive behaviour.

> Be polite and professional in your communication with learners.

> Convey confidence: stand tall and own the whole room; use your voice and gestures to convey your enthusiasm.

> Express your views and values, but accept learners' right to their views, even if you disagree with them.

> Give learners your full attention, focus on their NVC and listen actively with appropriate supportive NVC.

> Don't allow a learner to dominate, to constantly interrupt or talk when another learner is speaking.

> Try to avoid communicating when negative emotions such as anger or fear are in control.

> In a conflict situation stay calm, be open and positive, find out what the problem is, decide the best way to deal with it and be clear about your expectations.

Branching options

The following tasks are designed to help you consolidate and develop your communication skills to deter disruptions and to manage behaviour.

Reflection

Consider the sentence at the start of this chapter that stated, *One of the dominant fears that new teachers have is that some of their learners will disrupt their teaching.* To what extent is this true for your own experience, and do you still feel anxious about disruption? Reflect on how you have managed these feelings in your professional role and how you would advise other new teachers to deal with similar fears.

Analysis

Describe a recent incident when you were faced with challenging behaviour of one or more of your learners. How did you deal with this incident at the time? In the light of the guidance given in this chapter, would you act differently if faced with a similar situation in future? Note your conclusions and, if possible, compare your strategy with colleagues.

Research

I have quoted Carl Rogers' idea of *unconditional positive regard* as a concept that you can use to help you manage disruptive behaviour in your communication with learners. Use the literature to investigate this in more detail, and evaluate its relevance to your own teaching.

REFERENCES AND FURTHER READING

Lawrence, D (2000) *Building self-esteem with adult learners*. London: Paul Chapman Publishing.

McKay, M, Davis, M and Fanning, P (2009) *Messages: the communication skills book*. Oakland, CA: New Harbinger Publications Inc.

Race, P and Pickford, R (2007) *Making teaching work*. London: Sage Publications Ltd.

Rogers, C (1983) *Freedom to learn for the 80s*. New York: Macmillan.

Wallace, S (2007) *Managing behaviour in the lifelong learning sector*. Exeter: Learning Matters.

8
Communicating with large groups and with distance learners

This chapter will help you to:

- **communicate effectively with large groups of learners;**
- **communicate effectively with distance learners.**

Links to LLUK professional standards for QTLS:
AS3, AS4, AS7, AK3.1, AP3.1, AK4.2, AP4.2, BS2, BS3, BK1.2, BP1.2, BK2.2, BP2.2, BK3.1, BK3.2, BK3.3, BK3.4, BP3.1, BP3.2, BP3.3, BP3.4, CK3.4, CP3.4.

Links to CTLLS:
Unit 1 Preparing to teach in the lifelong learning sector;
Unit 2 Planning and enabling learning.

Links to DTLLS:
Unit 1 Preparing to teach in the lifelong learning sector;
Unit 2 Planning and enabling learning;
Unit 4 Theories and principles for planning and enabling learning;
Unit 5 Continuing personal and professional development;
Unit 6 Curriculum development for inclusive practice;
Unit 7 Wider professional practice.

Introduction

So far we have been looking mainly at interpersonal communication; interacting with learners face to face and, generally, on a one-to-one basis or with small groups of learners in a classroom. But this model isn't appropriate for every teaching situation; you may be interacting in settings with a large number of learners and you may be communicating with learners at a distance. These settings require a slightly different approach. For example, a lecture to a group of 50 or more learners would need to be delivered standing rather than sitting, as might be appropriate with fewer learners, and with distance learning there is greater emphasis on written communication. So, in this chapter we will look at the specific skills you will need for these two settings.

Interacting with a large group of learners

Large group activities include structured teaching sessions such as giving a lecture, a presentation or a demonstration. For the purpose of this section, we can define a large group as one greater than the normal maximum class size of around 30 people. Although communication fundamentals remain the same with a large group, there are some differences. Large group teaching is more tutor-centred and didactic, while small group teaching is more often learner-centred, with the tutor playing a mediating role and managing a considerable amount of learner participation. In addition, the atmosphere in a large group is less intimate and relaxed; for example, learners sometimes feel less comfortable asking and answering questions. Consequently, you are faced with situations that demand a different approach to communicating. In a large group:

- there is less scope for learners to participate, and for you to initiate and manage dialogue with each individual learner;
- there is less scope for learner–learner interaction;
- there is less scope for you to use a variety of communication strategies.

Anxiety

One issue which can dominate the thoughts of many trainee and newly qualified teachers is anxiety when facing a large audience. *Will I dry up? Will I mess it up? Will they like me? Will they be interested in what I'm saying? Will they even listen? What will they do?* Quite what we are frightened of will vary from person to person, but fear is extremely creative, conjuring up the worst nightmares of members of your audience heckling, walking out or falling asleep.

There are two points to bear in mind about anxiety. First, it's pretty normal to feel nervous, especially with an unfamiliar audience. Second, it's not necessarily a bad thing. Nerves bring an adrenaline surge that can keep us on our toes. In fact, even after many years of teaching, most teachers still get a nervous, excited buzz when meeting a new group. If the anxiety threatens to overwhelm you there are a number of things you can do to make it more manageable.

- Make sure you know what you are talking about. If it is a lecture, be sure you know your topic and practise delivering it. You could practise in front of a mirror or with a friend. You might even video yourself to pick up any obvious hiccups. Also, check that any equipment you are using is in working order.
- Visualise yourself going into that room full of people, greeting them, making eye contact and smiling. Imagine your voice calm and confident, and your body language positive and open. Do this a number of times. This is what athletes do before they perform and it really does improve their performance. Buzan (2001) explains why. If the mind has rehearsed many times, the body is also more prepared.
- Know your opening couple of sentences by heart. This will give you some breathing space to settle and to clear your mind.
- Try to find a few minutes beforehand to go through some relaxation techniques. Stand or sit quietly and clench and relax muscles in turn. This will help to keep you calm.
- Even if you are feeling extremely anxious, pretend that you are, in fact, that confident person who has no fears. Immediately before meeting an audience for the first time I used to imagine putting on the confident person's character, almost like donning a uniform. Try this out: put on the confident person's body language, for example standing up straight, looking ahead, making eye contact and smiling. Check that you are wearing the confident uniform as you enter the room. Remember, first impressions are very important. We are experts at identifying clues and making instinctive judgements. The audience will pick up confident body language and believe you to be confident.
- Another way to allay initial fears is to involve the audience immediately. This has the added advantage of helping to build rapport. You could ask them about their interest in the subject or what they know about it. Alternatively, you could give them a couple of statements about your topic and encourage them to

have a mini pre-talk discussion.

- It is natural to speak quickly when you are nervous. This is our fight or flight response instinctively urging us to get the whole thing over with as quickly as possible. But do the opposite; slow your voice down and pause often. Slowing down has a calming effect on the body.
- You might find a mind-map or prompt cards containing some key words or pictures helpful when you are speaking.

Delivering a lecture

We can illustrate the challenges of speaking to large groups with a practical situation.

CASE STUDY
Philosophically speaking

Scott is in the first year of DTLLS. So far, he's found it hard work but very enjoyable. He feels that he is doing reasonably well on the course but wants to make his lectures as interesting as possible. He thinks he might benefit from watching a professional lecturer and, hopefully, picking up some extra skills. A lecture on Stoic Philosophy is advertised locally and, although Scott knows nothing about either of the two speakers, he is quite interested in the subject, has bought a ticket and is now seated in the back row of a medium-sized room in the local guildhall.

It is about five minutes after the appointed time for the start of the lecture when the first speaker appears and walks up to a lectern placed towards the far corner at the front of the room (there is no stage). After a short *Good evening,* the speaker launches straight into his subject, *Greek Stoicism*, which takes Scott by surprise. The speaker's language is long-winded. He uses phrases such as, *It would seem to be the case that..* while Scott thinks it would make much more sense to say *It is...* But it's not just the words he is using, it's the way he is speaking that Scott finds so off-putting. His sentences seem to go on forever, without so much as a pause for breath. His voice is monotonous, lacking any variety, distinctly soporific, Scott thinks, as he battles against nodding off. It's as if the speaker isn't all that interested in his own subject. Scott notices that the speaker is reading most of the lecture and when he does look up he stares at the window at the end of the room. Scott also thinks that he has not moved from behind the lectern once during the lecture, although he's not too sure because he can't see all that well from the back row.

Scott is very thankful when, after about 30 minutes, the coffee break is announced. Initially, he feels that the only positive thing he has learnt from this speaker is don't make your lecture too long, but on reflection he realises that he's actually picked up a number of pointers about what not to do.

PRACTICAL TASK PRACTICAL TASK **PRACTICAL TASK** PRACTICAL TASK **PRACTICAL TASK**

What negative pointers did you pick up from this speaker? Note these and continue.

CASE STUDY
Still speaking philosophically

During the coffee break Scott chats to a number of people. Everyone seems very friendly and happy to talk. He notices one woman particularly because she has chatted to quite a few different groups of people during the fifteen-minute break.

After the coffee break Scott is not sure whether to stay for the second speaker, but he's paid his money so he might as well. When he returns to the lecture room he realises that the second speaker, standing at the front, is the woman who was chatting a lot in the break. The talk isn't due to begin for another couple of minutes but she is already talking to some of the people in the front row and they are all laughing. Dead on time she begins, saying *hello* to everyone as she smiles and looks around at the audience. She says a couple of things about herself and then starts on her talk, *The Roman Stoics*.

She begins by saying what the talk is about in a nutshell, then gives an outline of the main points. When she goes into detail about each point Scott is ready for it because she has already indicated what to expect. She speaks clearly, giving lots of interesting examples, sometimes speaking a little louder, sometimes putting more emphasis on certain words or parts of words. There's no doubt that she feels passionate about her subject; no chance of Scott nodding off here! Most of the time she speaks fairly slowly with quite a few pauses, where she looks expectantly around the room at everyone, including Scott, seated right at the back. He likes this because the pauses give him time to digest each point and her smile makes him feel included. It's as if she is looking to make sure everyone is interested and understands, as if she really values their reaction to her talk. *Perhaps she does,* Scott thinks. There are quite a few words that are unfamiliar to him but the speaker explains them carefully and most of them appear in the PowerPoint slide show she uses.

As the talk continues, Scott notices that the speaker has been moving about quite a bit, going to stand first at the end of the nearest couple of rows on one side of the room and then the other. He realises that he has a much better view of her than he had of the first speaker. Near the end of the talk she repeats all the major points and summarises them on her final PowerPoint slide. This helps to clarify a couple of things for Scott and reminds him of something that came up in class a couple of weeks ago. They were discussing different teaching strategies and someone suggested that in a lecture you should *Tell them what you're going to tell them, tell them, and then tell them what you've told them.*

Finally, the speaker thanks everyone for listening, says that she really enjoyed the session and that she would welcome some questions. Scott has also really enjoyed the session and his notebook is full of positive pointers for his own lectures.

PRACTICAL TASK PRACTICAL TASK **PRACTICAL TASK** PRACTICAL TASK **PRACTICAL TASK**

What positive pointers did you pick up from this speaker? Note these, and compare with the comments below on both speakers.

Of course, these two scenarios are extremes, although I can certainly recall attending a number of lectures very similar to the one delivered by the first speaker and thankfully many more similar to that delivered by the second speaker.

It's worth picking up on negative and positive pointers in these scenarios as a timely reminder of some dos and don'ts when talking to a large group of learners.

First Speaker

- Don't be late. Lateness tells the people in the audience that their time is not valuable. If possible, try to arrive a little early to greet everyone as they arrive.
- Try to avoid staying rooted to one spot and putting physical barriers (lecterns, desks, folded arms) between you and the audience.
- Don't use long-winded or passive language. It will sound boring and monotonous. Avoid unnecessary jargon and explain difficult words.
- Try to keep your sentences fairly short. Long sentences are difficult to follow.
- Try to avoid reading from notes. Using notes makes it difficult for you to engage with the audience as they are a barrier to maintaining eye contact. If you really need prompting, use prompt cards with key words or pictures, or a mind map of the main points.

Second Speaker

- Make sure you greet everyone. Make eye contact with the audience and smile. This will indicate that you are pleased to be there.
- Signpost your talk by using key words and phrases, such as *we've dealt with* ... and, *let's move on to* ..., and repeat important points. This helps with remembering and understanding.
- Speak clearly and slowly; pause often so that everyone has an opportunity to think about what you have said.
- Try to use interesting examples to make your talk more accessible.
- Vary the volume and tone of your voice to convey your enthusiasm. Good speakers are often able to keep their audience interested by emphasising, exaggerating and pausing.
- Visual aids, such as PowerPoint presentations, are an important element in increasing the impact and effectiveness of a lecture. However, they need to be used with sensitivity; this aspect is covered in more detail in Chapter 11.
- Focus on the people in the audience throughout to show that you are interested in their reaction and to check understanding. Some good speakers have the knack of appearing to talk to each person in an audience as an individual, as if they are having a private conversation with them.

You will recall that the second speaker encouraged the audience to ask questions. This is a useful strategy for clarifying important points and filling in information gaps, and someone may ask a question which is in the mind of a number of other members of the audience. However, inviting questions means that you have to be well prepared, and the best way to do this is to compile a list of possible questions beforehand. It's also a good idea to decide in advance whether you want to answer questions as they arise or at the end. You may wish to re-read the section on answering questions in Chapter 3.

Furniture arrangement

How the furniture is arranged for a large group is important, so important that no matter how good your skills, your lecture, presentation or demonstration might be compromised if the seating isn't appropriate. Yet it is often neglected and, in a large lecture theatre, you may well be restricted in changing the existing furniture arrangement. Nevertheless, there might be something you can do.

Let's return for a moment to Scott, attending the talk at the local guildhall.

PRACTICAL TASK PRACTICAL TASK **PRACTICAL TASK** PRACTICAL TASK **PRACTICAL TASK**

You will recall that Scott was able to see the second speaker because she moved around the room. Imagine you are that speaker but you are not able to move about the room. What could you do to ensure that everyone can see you?

There are two possibilities that you might consider. We know that Scott took a seat in the back row and we can assume from this that the room was pretty full. However, there is a good chance that it wasn't completely full; people will often sit in the back rows, even when there are a number of spaces dotted around, because they are reluctant to disturb those already seated. So you might consider saying that you would like everyone to be able to see you, and you them. Then you could ask those at the back to come and fill the empty seats. This is a worthy opening comment that tells the members of the audience that you are considering their needs. You might have to be persistent as people are sometimes reluctant to leave a seat that they have claimed as theirs.

If the room is completely full you might have a second option. We don't know whether the seating in the room was fixed but if not, it might be possible to move some of the seats forward. Of course, there might not be sufficient space and you would need to keep aisles free for health and safety requirements, but it is often an available option.

Interacting with learners at a distance

There is one area that brings a very specific set of problems to communicating with learners. This is flexible learning and, in particular, distance learning. Flexible learning is a term that has come to encompass a whole range of delivery techniques, including open learning (which refers to time), distance learning (which refers to place) and e-learning or online learning (which refers to the technology used to enable learning to happen). From the viewpoint of the tutor, there is one major feature of this type of learning which has a significant impact on communication style and effectiveness: the learners are remote. All the feedback you would normally receive from seeing a learner, interpreting their gestures, expressions and body language, is unavailable with learners who are only accessible via a telephone or a computer screen and may be hundreds, or even thousands, of miles away.

So how can you communicate effectively in these circumstances? This is important because it is a growth area. In the UK, distance learning courses have been available for over half a century and the Open University, in operation since 1970, is now the biggest university in Europe. Increasingly, colleges and training organisations are investigating ways of attracting learners who cannot undertake traditional courses that require regular attendance at a particular site, over an extended period of time. Many colleges now have a range of courses that are delivered substantially online, or you may just find yourself having to support a learner who is moving away from the local area and wishes to complete their traditional programme in a distance learning mode.

Distance learning has some inherent disadvantages. Kirkup and Jones list these as:

- *inability to offer dialogue in the way that a face-to-face... educational ideal might;*
- *the isolation and individualisation of the student.*

(Kirkup and Jones, in Raggart et al, 1996, p277)

These limitations can be mitigated by effective communication between tutor and learners (or exaggerated if this communication is ineffective). So the task for distance learning tutors is to communicate with their learners to make them feel understood, valued, supported and part of a learning community. Let us see how this might work in practice.

Establishing an effective communication process with distance learners

PRACTICAL TASK PRACTICAL TASK **PRACTICAL TASK** PRACTICAL TASK **PRACTICAL TASK**

One of your learners is about to move to a different part of the country, and you have agreed to support her for the final six months of her second year course by tutoring her in a distance learning mode. You need to establish an agreement on the practicalities of communicating with each other. What do you think should be included? Note the important points and compare with the suggestions below.

This agreement essentially forms part of a learning contract, agreed between you and your learner, so that you both know and understand the communication process that you will use. I think it should include:

- a provisional schedule to include what course material you will provide and when and how it will be sent;
- the communication equipment that you will both use and details of your learner's internet access;
- arrangements if there is an emergency or difficulty in communicating online;
- response times for e-mails;
- response times for giving constructive and detailed feedback on coursework;
- when and how contact will be made.

Such an agreement is essential in distance learning. It avoids false expectations on the part of the learner, and both parties are clear on how they will communicate to make the course a success.

In this task you had a significant advantage in deciding how to communicate with your learner in the distance learning mode: you knew her. You had built up a relationship over 18 months, established personal rapport and knew your learner as an individual, with all her foibles, strengths and weaknesses. This is a luxury that many distance learning tutors don't have. Many will never, or rarely, meet their learners, and so the learners' relationship with them is determined almost entirely by communication at a distance. And predominantly, this is likely to be written communication: course books, handouts, assignment briefing sheets, e-mails, assessments and so on. If you are in this situation, you may be lucky enough to speak on the phone or to meet occasionally, at enrolment, induction or the occasional tutorial, but most likely it is your writing that will determine the relationship between you and your distance learners.

So what sort of relationship with your distance learners should you be looking for and how best can you present yourself to achieve it? If we can define this, it should give us pointers as to how we write to them.

REFLECTIVE TASK

REFLECTIVE TASK

Imagine you are going to enrol on a distance learning version of a course in your subject area. What qualities do you think are important in your tutor in order that you can gain the maximum benefit from their support?

I tried this task with some of my own learners. The most common responses were as follows:

Sympathy; knows his subject; reliability; marks assignments on time; friendly; understands when I can't get work done; keeps in contact; tells me where I have gone wrong and how to put it right; addresses me by my first name; is clear about how to contact him; acknowledges my e-mails; does what he says he will do; doesn't mess me about; has a personal and friendly touch (enjoy your holiday); is interested in me; writes and spells correctly; shows the human touch.

I think it is possible to establish a relationship that encompasses most of these qualities even though you may never meet your learners face-to-face. One thing is certain: the initial contact will go a long way to determining the nature of this relationship, and this is often done in a tutor's welcome e-mail or letter to a newly enrolled learner. Such a message can encourage and motivate a new learner or, at the other extreme, frighten the living daylights out of them and reinforce a whole series of negative prejudices about the academic world. Let's look at this in practice.

CASE STUDY
The new distance learner
Sarah is a newly enrolled learner on a distance learning course at Branton College. From her application, her tutor knows she is a single mother who has done no academic study for four years, when she left a college course prematurely without taking her exam. Her academic record shows that she should be capable of succeeding at this level, but this is her first distance learning course. A week before the course is due to start, she receives the following welcome e-mail:

From: a.pedant@brantoncollege.ac.uk
To: s.patterson@hotmail.co.uk
Subject: Online course at Branton College
Date: 23 September

Dear Ms Paterson

Thank you for enrolling on the creative writing course at Branton College. My name is Dr Andrew Pedant, and I have been appointed as your tutor for the course. My duties are to ensure you receive all the course materials and to answer any queries you may have as you work your way through the course booklets. I am also responsible for marking your TMAs (Tutor Marked Assignments), which occur at regular intervals through the programme.

You will receive the first module within the next few days, together with details of your user name, password and instructions on how to log on and access the course materials. Please acknowledge receipt. I believe the materials are self-explanatory, but I am available to answer any questions you may have every Thursday afternoon between 2.00 and 4.30pm during term time. You can contact me, or my secretary on 01235-687349.

I hope to contact you in about two weeks' time to check your progress. Meanwhile I wish you well with the course, which I am sure you will find challenging and worthwhile.

Sincerely

Andrew Pedant (Dr)
Creative Writing Course Director

PRACTICAL TASK PRACTICAL TASK **PRACTICAL TASK** PRACTICAL TASK **PRACTICAL TASK**

How would you feel if you received this message? Note your reaction and list any suggestions you would offer to the tutor to improve his welcome e-mail.

Although the content of this message is undoubtedly accurate, there are many things about it that would certainly discourage me as a potential learner. Here are some of the comments I would make.

- The e-mail doesn't appear to have been written by an approachable and friendly person. The tone is peremptory (*Please acknowledge receipt*), unwelcoming (does not even say *Welcome to the course*) and arrogant (*I believe the materials are self-explanatory*).
- There are no personal touches: it reads like a standard e-mail sent out to all new learners, and in this case Sarah's surname is even spelt wrongly.
- Barriers are being set up, both in terms of status (emphasis on *Dr* and job title) and of access (limited times available for advice).
- There is no evidence of understanding of Sarah's unfamiliarity with online learning, or her potential anxiety at being away from education for four years and being able to pass the course.
- The overall impression created by the message is threatening rather than encouraging. For example, the focus on assignments at this early stage, and the promise to check progress, would certainly not boost my confidence as a new and anxious learner.

Now compare Dr Pedant's message with the following:

From: m.paffey@brantoncollege.ac.uk
To: s.patterson@hotmail.co.uk
Subject: Welcome to your Creative Writing course
Date: 10 September

Hello Sarah

Thank you for enrolling on the Creative Writing course and welcome to the programme.

I am pleased to have been appointed as your tutor. My name is Maurice Paffey, and I have been working as a Lecturer in English at Branton College for the last 10 years. Three years ago, I helped to design the online Creative Writing course, and have enjoyed being a tutor on the programme ever since then.

The course will begin formally on 1 October, and I will send you full details of how to log on and access the course materials a few days before then. I know that online learning can be a bit frightening if you haven't studied like this before, and that everything will feel new and unfamiliar. So please contact me at any time with any queries you may have, no matter how trivial they may appear. If you send me an e-mail I will try to reply within 48 hours. If this is difficult you can reach me by phoning 01235-687349. Even if I am not available, please leave a message and I will get back to you as soon as I can.

I see from your enrolment form that you have already had articles published in a local magazine. You must tell me more about this sometime soon; I always enjoy discussions with a fellow writer. Meanwhile, I do hope you enjoy the course, and I am looking forward to working with you during the next year.

Please could you reply to this email so that I know that we are really in contact? And don't forget to get in touch with me if you have any questions.

Best wishes

Maurice

REFLECTIVE TASK

By comparing the two e-mails above, consider the main features that you would wish to embed in your communication with distance learners, in order to establish and maintain an effective and supportive relationship.

Communicating with distance learning groups

So far we have only been considering communication between a tutor and one distance learner. However, it is possible that you might be involved in supporting a group of learners (although possibly at different points of the course at any one time), and that these learners may have the facility to communicate with each other. Welcome to the world of electronic study groups and conferencing. This brings a set of communication issues for you to consider in addition to the one-to-one model we have been dealing with to date. Here are some of them.

- There is likely to be considerable variation in your learners' ICT skills and confidence. Some learners may be expert and have previous conferencing experience; some may be novices. In any event, you need to provide time and support for learners to familiarise themselves with your system of communication.
- Some of your learners may be unfamiliar with e-mail conventions and practice. You will need to establish and agree with your learners the conventions that you wish to apply in communicating with the group, for example on netiqette (net etiquette), log on times and so on. More detailed guidance on this is given in the following section.

- Some learners may be shy. Be aware that some learners may be reluctant to contribute at an early stage of the course; gentle encouragement may be needed.
- ...and some may be aggressive and insensitive. In this case, some tactful advice may be required.
- Some discussions may go off track (or struggle to survive). Be prepared to lead or facilitate discussion by judicious use of questioning, encouragement, praise and use of learners' names.

These points are a very brief introduction to e-communication with groups, but the topic is well covered in the literature. In particular, Julia Duggleby's, *How to be an online tutor* and Gilly Salmon's, *E-moderating* give comprehensive coverage of the work of an online tutor.

Communicating by e-mail

It is likely that much of your communication with distance learners will be via e-mail. It is important that your own e-mail etiquette is good, and that you encourage your learners to abide by the accepted conventions. In this way, you minimise the chance of messages being misinterpreted when you don't have the luxury of visual and immediate feedback through body language, gesture and verbal response.

Let us look at an e-mail message that ignores some of these conventions: our old friend Andrew Pedant is at work again.

From: a.pedant@brantoncollege.ac.uk
To: s.patterson@hotmail.co.uk
Cc: j.lineman@brantoncollege.ac.uk
Subject: Assignment
Date: 12 March

Dear Sarah

Where is you assignment? It should have been submitted FIVE days ago!!!

Please could you let me know when I am likely to receive it? I'll then be able to take it with me on my holiday as light reading!

Also, I would like to arrange a date for our next tutorial. Can I suggest next Thursday at 3.00pm in my new office (map attached)? And thank you for your request for an extension for the Module 3 TMA – I'll let you know the decision in due course.

Yours

Andrew

PRACTICAL TASK PRACTICAL TASK **PRACTICAL TASK** PRACTICAL TASK **PRACTICAL TASK**

List any breaches of e-mail etiquette that you can identify in this message and compare with the following comments.

The important thing to realise about this type of e-mail is that it is a formal type of communication and should conform to the normal rules of formal writing. It isn't an informal chat between friends, especially not of the text talk variety such as *Hi, do u fncy mtn up 4 a d8 l8r?* In this respect Andrew's e-mail is not too bad, although he should have picked up the typo in the first sentence. However, he still has not learnt much about adopting a friendly tone and many of the conventions have been ignored. Clarke (2009, pp60–3) contains a good section on how e-mails should be written, and here is my selection of top tips.

- Use precise titles. 'Assignment' is too vague. Which assignment? And even, which course?
- Be respectful of privacy. Who is Mr Lineman and why has he been copied into this message? Sarah will probably be none too pleased that a third party is included in such a critically phrased message.
- Don't use capitals (*FIVE*). This is equivalent to shouting and is very discourteous.
- Don't over-use punctuation marks (!!!).
- Use humour and smileys sparingly: the heavy-handed attempt here is not likely to provoke much laughter, particularly in view of the critical content of the message.
- Avoid multiple topics in one e-mail. Two distinct new topics have been introduced into the final paragraph. They would have been better sent as separate messages.
- Don't send a message when you are angry; calm down before you press the *Send* button. If you don't, the reaction of the recipient may not be what you want, and you may well regret it later.

All this is a bit negative, so here are the key points to remember.

- Know what your organisation's e-mail policy is, and abide by it.
- Use correct grammar and spelling.
- Think of your recipient; treat them with politeness and respect.
- Use precise titles and limit your e-mail to one topic alone: one topic, one e-mail.
- Check your message before you press *Send.*

A SUMMARY OF **KEY POINTS**

> **Anxiety is normal when facing a large group for the first time, but there are a number of helpful strategies to manage it.**

> **Simple presentation skills, such as maintaining eye contact, showing enthusiasm and speaking clearly, are just as important when communicating with a large group.**

> **Communication can be improved if furniture is arranged to encourage eye contact with the speaker.**

> **Distance learning tutors need to communicate with their learners in a way that makes them feel understood, valued and supported.**

> **In distance learning, the most important form of communication is likely to be written communication; it should reflect the supportive and professional role of the tutor.**

> **E-mail correspondence should be professional and sensitive to the needs of the learner.**

Branching options

The following tasks are designed to help you consolidate and develop the learning points covered in this chapter.

Reflection

When you next give a demonstration, presentation or lecture to a large group, focus on the behaviour of your audience. Note those occasions where they signal that they are particularly interested, and those when they appear less so. Try to identify reasons for this, and note your conclusions in your journal.

Analysis

Review the e-mails that you have sent to your learners recently, and analyse the extent to which they conform to the guidelines for good practice given in the section *Communicating by e-mail* above. Note your conclusions.

Research

Investigate the concept of online learning, from the standpoint of how this affects the role of tutors in communicating with their learners. The books by Gilly Salmon and Julia Duggleby, detailed below, may provide a good starting point for this research.

REFERENCES AND FURTHER READING REFERENCES AND FURTHER READING

Buzan, T (2001) *Head Strong.* London: Thorsons.

Clarke, A (2009) *The minimum core for information and communication technology*. Exeter: Learning Matters.

Duggleby, J (2000) *How to be an online tutor*. Aldershot: Gower Publishing Company.

Raggart, P et al (1996) *The learning society.* London: Routledge.

Salmon, G (2000) *E-moderating*. London: Kogan Page.

Websites

www.open.ac.uk
www.nocn.org.uk

9
Communicating within organisations

This chapter will help you to:

- understand how the ethos of an organisation affects communication within it;
- identify the ethos and characteristics of communication in your organisation;
- identify your communication network and role set within your organisation;
- identify and analyse appropriate communication styles in communicating with colleagues.

Links to LLUK professional standards for QTLS:

AS3, AS4, AS5, AS7, AK4.1, AK4.2, AP4.1, AP4.2, AK5.1, AK5.2, AP5.1, AP5.2, BS2, BK1.2, BP1.2, BK3.1, BK3.4, BK3.5, BP3.1, BP3.4, BP3.5, EK2.4, EP2.4, EK5.3, EP5.3, FK4.2, FP4.2.

Links to CTLLS:

Unit 2 Planning and enabling learning.

Links to DTLLS:

Unit 2 Planning and enabling learning;

Unit 4 Theories and principles for planning and enabling learning;

Unit 5 Continuing personal and professional development;

Unit 7 Wider professional practice.

Introduction

The main focus of this book concerns communication between teachers and learners in the lifelong learning sector. But this isn't the whole story because learning doesn't take place in some idealistic environment where there are no interruptions, no frustrations and no awkward, and sometimes downright antagonistic, colleagues. Although the sector is incredibly diverse, varying from massive multi-site organisations with thousands of learners to small education centres with a handful of learners and teachers, the common factor is that these are all organisations full of people, and these people are communicating with each other. The quality and effectiveness of this communication will have a direct effect on the quality of learning in the classroom, and the quality of a teacher's professional life.

So this chapter looks at the nature of organisations and their communication systems, and applies these concepts to the role of teachers in the lifelong learning sector. This leads to an investigation of how you can identify your own communication network and style to gain maximum benefit for your learners, to say nothing of your own well-being and sanity!

Ethos of organisations

There is no doubt that the ethos of an organisation has a direct effect on how people within it communicate with each other. For example, if you work within a traditionally structured organisation, with clear departmental lines of responsibility and an autocratic management, you probably won't communicate in the same way as in an organisation with a less rigid structure and management style. So let's start by looking at this concept of organisational ethos.

There is a wealth of research on organisational cultures and how they affect the individuals who work within them. One of the best known is the work of Charles Handy (1976). He identified four main cultures, which he called role, task, person and power. Let's look at each of these in turn.

The role culture

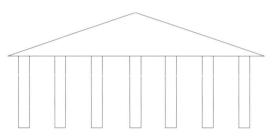

The role culture is usually depicted as a temple, where the pillars represent departments controlled by a powerful senior management group. In this culture the main features are:

- the importance of roles, as defined by written job descriptions;
- well-defined rules and procedures for managing the organisation;
- a tendency to be impersonal, with individuals seeming to be less important than the posts they occupy.

If you work in an organisation that is structured in a traditional way, with curriculum-based departments co-ordinated and directed by a senior management team, you may find evidence of a role culture in operation.

The task culture

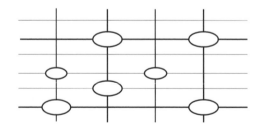

The task culture is much more flexible than the role culture, and is usually depicted as a network which shows task groups and the connections between them. Here the main features are:

- high priority given to achieving specific tasks;
- a high value given to personal expertise;
- a flexible organisation of specialist teams that are formed for specific tasks and disperse when the job is done.

If you work in an organisation that has project/task teams and cross-college co-ordinating departments, it is probable that it has a strong element of the task culture.

The person culture

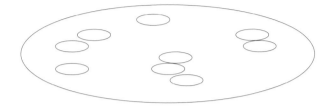

The person culture is shown as a group of individuals who, for mutual benefit, work within one organisation. In this culture:

- the individual is paramount; people are in the organisation to develop and use their expertise;
- the organisation is subordinate, and exists to provide facilities and support to the individual members;
- influence depends on expertise.

In educational organisations this is perhaps most often seen in some universities, which cherish the fact that world-famous professors and leading-edge research exist in particular faculties.

The power culture

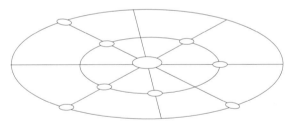

Finally, the power culture is drawn as a web, which represents key individuals located at strategic points within the web. The main features are:

- power being exercised by influential individuals whose power usually stems from control of resources;
- a competitive atmosphere;
- individuals being judged primarily by results.

You may have come across this in small college sites or departments where the head of department runs the department as some sort of personal fiefdom through charisma, resource control or just by having been there for a long time.

REFLECTIVE TASK
~~REFLECTIVE TASK~~

Consider your own organisation. To what extent does it conform to one or other of the role, task, person and power cultures?

Organisational cultures in educational organisations

Handy recognised that organisations don't fall neatly into one or other of these four categories, but argued that it is often possible to identify a tendency towards one culture or a combination of cultures in most work organisations. I have come across all four cultures in colleges, training centres and universities. I have worked in a college where people have argued that moving a piece of equipment from one room to another had to by done by a technician because it was in their job description and not mine. Similarly, in another college I have been appointed to so many teams operating simultaneously that I have had difficulty in remembering whether the lunchtime meeting was about course evaluation, publicity visits to local schools or planning for next year's enrolment!

There are many reasons why an organisation may exhibit a tendency towards a particular culture. It may be because of the character and management style of the Principal or senior executive. An autocratic style is likely to generate a very different ethos and culture to that of a democratic management style, which puts an emphasis on participation and consultation. Hewton (cited in Boyd-Barrett et al, 1983) suggests that the nature of different subjects tends to create distinctive cultures even within a single organisation, and I have experienced college departments that fit this pattern. For instance, I have worked in a department with a raft of humanities disciplines which conformed to a much more democratic ethos than the neighbouring engineering department which was more interested in clarity and getting the job done. Another likely determinant is history and tradition, particularly if there are holders of key posts who have spent their whole working lives in the organisation and see themselves as responsible for maintaining what they regard as valuable organisational traditions. In any event, if you wish to communicate effectively in your professional role, it is useful to identify the culture of your own organisation and your particular work area.

In 1976, Handy was writing about commercial and industrial organisations. One of his later books, written with Robert Aitken (Handy and Aitken, 1986), applied these ideas to secondary schools, and it seems reasonable that their conclusions may also be applicable to universities, colleges and other post-16 organisations. They concluded that these organisations exhibited:

> *a predominance of the role culture. They were big, the work-flow was very interdependent, with the timetable or operations plan a major feature, responsibility was divided up by function (academic and pastoral, year tutor or subject teacher), and there were arrays of systems, co-ordinating procedures and committee meetings ... Within the role culture however a person culture bubbles away. The privacy of the classroom, the right to express one's own views in one's own way and the sense of accountability to one's profession – these are all hallmarks of a profession and of a person culture.*

> (Handy and Aitken, 1986, pp93–4)

I wonder whether you feel that these conclusions would be valid for your organisation?

Communication systems in organisations

Just as it's possible to categorise organisational cultures, it is also possible to categorise communication systems in organisations. Let's look at formal and informal systems and at grapevines.

Formal and informal communication systems

Formal systems are the official communication channels in an organisation. Typically, they will include written communications, such as staff handbooks, management directives, letters, minutes of meetings, college policies, newsletters, timetables, maps, signs and so on. They will also include recorded oral communication through meetings, interviews, appraisals and formal face-to-face discussions. Of these, meetings are likely to take up much of your time, whether they be regular staff meetings, meetings with parents and employers, examination boards, committee meetings, team meetings and so on *ad infinitum*. So there is no shortage of methods and forums through which communication can take place in educational organisations.

These formal systems can also be seen in terms of the direction of communication flow, that is either vertically, horizontally or diagonally. Vertical communication represents the information passed from senior management downwards and the responses passing back upwards, tracing the authority line of the organisation. Thus, a memo to all department heads asking for data on staff holiday plans and the resulting returns will fall into this category. Similarly, each department will have a vertical chain of communication of its own. Horizontal communication is that which flows between departments across the organisation, such as an e-mail from one departmental head to another concerning sharing room arrangements. Typically, the further down the line of authority you go, the less horizontal communication you will find. The result is that staff in one department may have little idea what their colleagues in other departments are doing. Diagonal or complex communication also crosses departmental lines, but is between people of different status in the organisation, such as a request from a senior lecturer to a technician in the IT unit for an additional software package to be installed.

Informal systems include the routine discussions, telephone conversations, face-to-face chats, notes left on desks and e-mails between colleagues which occur throughout every working day. They seldom form part of the official communication records that end up on college files, but they form a considerable part of the overall communication that takes place in an organisation's daily life.

PRACTICAL TASK PRACTICAL TASK **PRACTICAL TASK** PRACTICAL TASK **PRACTICAL TASK**

In your organisation, how would you expect to receive the following information (and from whom)?

- A last-minute change in your timetable.
- Notice of a proposed Ofsted inspection.
- An amendment to the organisation's disciplinary procedures.
- Cancellation of this afternoon's course team meeting.
- Arrangements for next year's enrolments.

- A complaint from the refectory about one of your learners.
- News of tentative negotiations for a merger with a nearby college;
- Plans for your course as written in the five-year plan.

In my case, most of these pieces of information came in the manner you would expect: phone messages, face-to-face chat, e-mails and memos. The exceptions were the ones about disciplinary procedures and course plans (not received at all, but discovered coincidentally), and the merger rumour, which I first heard about by reading it in the local newspaper!

When you review your response to this task, try to identify those messages that would form part of the formal communication processes, and those that you would classify as informal. Do these messages use the most appropriate channels of communication? If practicable, compare your responses with a colleague from another organisation or another department in your organisation.

Grapevines

Information doesn't always flow smoothly through these formal and informal channels. This is where grapevines appear and flourish. You can see grapevines in action in coffee room chats, conversations in the local pub, passing the time at the photocopying machine, sharing the latest gossip as you meet a colleague in the corridor. There is always a grapevine in an organisation. It seems that where formal systems in an organisation do not function effectively, the grapevine will prosper.

The grapevine may be inevitable, but not necessarily a bad thing. It can give people a sense of belonging, of feeling part of a team or group with a common purpose and value. However, grapevine gossip and rumour certainly can be destructive and upsetting, and have a negative effect on morale and atmosphere in any organisation. Here is Jason, talking about his experience of college grapevines, firstly in his present college where he is a senior lecturer in construction crafts, and then in his first appointment.

Grapevine? Oh yes, we certainly have one of those. Our grapevine is called Margaret, one of our technicians. Margaret has been in the college for about 30 years, knows everyone, has worked in nearly every department, and is the sort of person who is really interested in people. The college is her life and she loves it. She seems to get advance information of anything that's going to happen and who is coming and going. None of her gossip is malicious because she genuinely likes people and they seem to confide in her. So, all in all, it's a good grapevine for us as a department, like when she heard that the college was going to have a couple of all-dancing all-singing photocopiers on trial, so my boss managed to get in quick and have one allocated to our staff room.

Mind you, when I started teaching we had an awful grapevine. I was a part-timer working in a big rural college, but at a small centre in a town about eight miles from the main site. One day we heard a rumour that the college had overspent by about half a million pounds and was going to have to make cuts. By the end of the week, everyone was saying that our site would have to be sold, our courses would not run next year and we would all be redundant. The thing was that I really needed that job, and didn't know how I could cope if I lost it. So I had about six weeks of sleepless nights, not daring to ask about my job officially in case I upset somebody. In fact, the college wasn't in debt, not by so much anyway, and I even managed to get a full-time appointment the following year, but I wouldn't want to go through all that trauma again, and we never did find out how the rumour started.

REFLECTIVE TASK

Consider the nature of the grapevine in your organisation. Can you think of any examples of where it has been beneficial or harmful to your learners? How do you feel grapevine rumour or gossip is best dealt with when you believe it might affect you or your learners?

Communication roles in the lifelong learning sector

So far we have been looking at the organisation; it is now time to turn to your professional role, in particular to look at how this role is enacted through communication with others.

Roles and role sets

The first question is, *Which others*? The answer is everyone who you come into contact with while doing your job, in addition to your learners. And this can form a large and diverse number of people, all of whom are playing out their own work roles, have definite expectations of the way you will communicate with them, and are very conscious of their own place within the organisation. I asked a group of trainee teachers to record who they communicated with at work over the period of one week, and how often contact was made with each one. The result looked something like this; the most frequent contacts appear first, the least frequent last.

Other lecturers teaching the same courses
Other lecturers using the same staffroom
Departmental admin staff
College technicians
Library staff
Head of Department's secretary
College Admin office staff
Refectory staff
Caretakers
Line manager
Friends from other departments (mainly lecturers)
Employers and parents

In addition, there were some contacts that were infrequent, but perceived as important. These included external verifiers, Ofsted inspectors, the college Principal, other senior managers and external examiners.

One way of classifying this network of people is through the idea of a role set. This is a term used by social psychologists involved in role theory, and has been well defined by Hartley.

> *No role exists in isolation. For any given role, usually called the focal role, there are*
> *a number of other roles related to it ... These are called the role set ... The most*

important thing about these roles is that each one makes demands upon the focal role.

(Hartley, 1999, p119)

This leads to the idea of role conflict, particularly where the numerous roles we all enact come into conflict. For example, if you are a parent, this role can conflict with your role at work if your child is sick. In the present context we are limiting the discussion to work roles, and role set analysis is a very useful tool to analyse individual communication networks. Your role set can be depicted as a diagram. For illustration, here is the role set diagram of Jean Paul, a part-time lecturer in French, who teaches three classes a week at his local college.

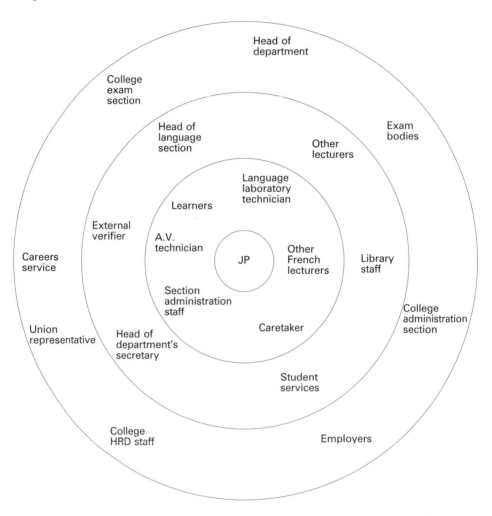

In this diagram, Jean Paul has indicated the importance he attaches to others in his role set by the distance away from his own circle; the further away, the less significant. There are other ways of indicating significance; size of circle, colour coding, etc.; it's your choice. The important thing is to get some idea of the complexity and scope of the role and of the communication network in which you operate as a matter of daily routine.

PRACTICAL TASK PRACTICAL TASK **PRACTICAL TASK** PRACTICAL TASK **PRACTICAL TASK**

Draw a role set diagram for yourself in your professional role. Compare the result with the role set of one or more colleagues and note any significant similarities and differences.

Roles and communication styles

Having identified who you communicate with, the next stage is to consider your communication style. For example, do you use the same style when talking to an external examiner as you do with your colleague who teaches the same learners as you do?

It is likely that when you are at work you treat others not only on the basis of their personality, but also on your view of the job they are doing. If the college Principal walked into your staff room for a coffee and chat, my guess is that the atmosphere and dialogue would differ significantly from what you would expect if the department administrative assistant did the same thing. You are seeing the job personified, or the role, as well as the individual.

So people at work are very conscious of their roles, and communicate in what they see as a manner that fits this role. Not only that, but we expect others to act out their roles and communicate in an appropriate way. Peeke (1980) sees roles as subject to three sets of perceptions.

> *In joining any organisation we enter the role system of that organisation. One set [of perceptions] is that of the organisation...an ascribed role with a set of behaviours often identified in a job description. Another set is identified by those who interact with the occupant of the role. The third set of perceptions are those of the occupant of the role.*

(Peeke, 1980, p77)

In any work situation, therefore, in addition to your own idea of how to communicate at work, the organisation as a whole has expectations as to how you will do your job; so do all the people you communicate with. Problems tend to arise when these expectations are not met and this can be reflected in the communication process.

Occasionally you can find traces of academic arrogance in educational organisations, where some academic staff tend to use the organisation as though they are the key high-status figures and the rest of the organisation (administrators, technicians, etc.) is there to support them; shades of the person culture. If this attitude is reflected in their communication style, problems can arise. Here is one.

CASE STUDY
Alistair's story

Alistair is the site supervisor at the city-centre site of a large college, housing the college's Health and Social Studies department. Here he is talking about his job.

It's not too bad a job really, and most of the staff are OK. Especially Frances (the Head of Department), who is a pleasure to work for. Always says Hello, *asks after the wife and kids, always invites us to the Christmas party, and always has time to listen to me if I've a problem. Like last week, when one of the BTEC First Diploma groups left all sorts of food wrappers and drink bottles in room six, in spite of the* No food in classroom *rules. Her door's always open, and she listened to my moans even though I knew she was due to go and see the Marketing Director. The thing is, she treats you like a real person who's got an important job to do, and you always feel she is really interested in what you've got to say. So I'd do a lot for her, like last summer when I heard that Nixon's bookshop next door was moving and had some spare office furniture they wanted to get rid of. Told Frances, and she managed to upgrade the staffroom on the basis of that tip.*

So I wish they were all like her. Actually most of them are fine and it's a happy place to work, apart from the odd one or two. The worst is the new bloke that started in September, Dr Jones, as he likes to be called. He just treats us like we don't exist most of the time, and when he does see us it's as though we were some sort of servant! Arrives in the morning and the best you can get out of him is a grunt. If he wants anything it's a memo and very brusque. Please make sure that there is a flip chart in room 5 at 9.00 tomorrow morning! *That's not even my job, it's Jim's (the technician). And he's just as rude to Lorna (our admin assistant) – told her off no end the other day for being late with his photocopying, and we all heard him. So I don't think many of us will be in a hurry to help him out next month when he's setting up his exhibition for Open Day.*

PRACTICAL TASK PRACTICAL TASK **PRACTICAL TASK** PRACTICAL TASK **PRACTICAL TASK**

What can you learn from Alistair's story concerning your own communication style as a teacher working in an educational organisation? Note anything you should do or avoid doing. Over the next month or so at work, see if you can identify any changes.

Beyond the obvious practical things that come from this case study, like not criticising someone while others are within earshot, this scenario raises a couple of important general points. The insensitive communication style depicted here occurs in all organisations. It is likely to be prevalent in role cultures because of the hierarchical nature of this ethos, in power cultures because of the competitive ethos here, and in person cultures if the *star* performers see themselves as superior to the rest of the staff. Even in task cultures, a tendency to see the task groups as more important than the rest of the organisation's activities can encourage an attitude that values some staff less than others.

The insensitivity is often a consequence of defining people entirely by their role, rather than seeing them as individuals. So Liz Smith tends to gets deferential treatment if she is the Curriculum Director, and gets ignored if she is the cleaner who looks after the top floor of your building. If we can somehow see people at work as individuals, whose personality is much more than the role they are enacting, then this is a good start to communicating with them in a way that makes them feel valued, and they will respond accordingly. A good example of this is shown in the attitude of Derrick, a director in a large training organisation. Here he explains his approach.

There used to be a fashionable management theory called MBO – Management by Objectives. Well I call my style MBWA – Management by Walking About. For at least half an hour each day, I wander around the place, dropping in to staffrooms and talking to people there and in corridors. You wouldn't believe how many problems I've nipped in the bud just by being available and approachable to people who take the chance to have a chat informally, but who would never have come to disturb me in my office.

One thing is for sure. An insensitive communication style towards colleagues will be counter-productive, and produce resentment which will make co-operation difficult in future. In the case study, Dr Jones may well take hours in setting up his Open Day display because help from others is grudging or non-existent. In our professional life, our learners will be disadvantaged if our colleagues see us as another Dr Jones.

A SUMMARY OF **KEY POINTS**

> **Organisations have distinctive cultures that can be characterised as role, task, person and power cultures.**

> **The communication system of an organisation can be influenced by the predominant culture of that organisation.**

> **Your professional role is enacted through the way you communicate, not only with your learners, but also with other members of your role set.**

> **Your communication style needs to take account of the sensitivities of others.**

Branching options

The following tasks are designed to help you consolidate and develop the learning points covered in this chapter.

Reflection

Consider the potential for conflict within your role set and the strategies you might be able to employ to resolve them.

Analysis

Select three or four people from your role set who work in your organisation. Analyse the communication style you use with each one, and note differences and similarities. Note why you use a different style with different colleagues.

Research

Peter Senge and Malcolm Tight, among others, have written about *the learning organisation.* Use the internet and your library to investigate this concept. To what extent do you feel that an organisation you are familiar with exhibits the characteristics of a learning organisation? Is there any evidence that these characteristics are reflected in the way people in the organisation communicate with one another?

REFERENCES AND FURTHER READING

Boyd-Barrett, O et al (1983) *Approaches to post-school management*. London: Harper and Row.

Evans, D (2000) *People, communication and organisations*. Basingstoke: Longman.

Handy, C (1993) *Understanding organisations*. London: Penguin.

Handy, C and Aitken, R (1986) *Understanding schools as organisations*. London: Penguin.

Hartley, P (1999) *Interpersonal communication*. London: Routledge.

Peeke, G (1980) Role strain in the further education college, *The Vocational Aspects of Education, vol.XXXII,* no. 83: 77–80.

Raggat, P et al (1996) *The learning society*. London: Routledge.

Senge, P (2006) *The fifth discipline: the art and practice of the learning organisation*. London: Random House.

Tight, M (1996) *Key concepts in adult education and training*. London: Routledge.

10
Communicating with colleagues

This chapter will help you to:

- establish and maintain effective interpersonal communication with colleagues;
- communicate effectively in group and team situations;
- resolve communication problems with colleagues.

Links to LLUK professional standards for QTLS:

AS3, AS4, AS5, AS7, AK4.2, AP4.2, AK5.1, AK5.2, AP5.1, AP5.2, BS2, BK1.2, BP1.2, BK3.1, BK3.4, BK3.5, BP3.1, BP3.4, BP3.5, DK3.2, DP3.2, EK2.4, EP2.4, EK5.3, EP5.3, FK4.2, FP4.2.

Links to CTLLS:

Unit 2 Planning and enabling learning.

Links to DTLLS:

Unit 2 Planning and enabling learning;

Unit 4 Theories and principles for planning and enabling learning;

Unit 5 Continuing personal and professional development;

Unit 7 Wider professional practice.

Introduction

If your learners' experience of study in your organisation is to be rewarding and successful, you will need to communicate and collaborate with colleagues, employers, moderators and many others to ensure your learners get the best deal. This has been recognised in the LLUK standards in several places, notably in Domain A, *Professional values and practice*, for example in AP5.1, which states that teachers need to:

> communicate and collaborate with colleagues and/or others within and outside the organisation, to enhance learners' experience.

> (LLUK, 2006, p4)

It is likely that you will spend as much time communicating with colleagues as you do with your learners. First, you will receive and send messages to colleagues throughout your working day, as a matter of routine. Second, you will discuss issues with colleagues in formal settings such as interviews and meetings or informally in the staff room. Finally, you will be involved in group communication, either as a group member or perhaps as a group leader. You will probably be involved in course teams, in academic committees, in exam boards and inevitably you will attend meetings. This chapter considers the communication skills that are needed to survive and prosper in this arena.

Receiving and sending information

We saw in the previous chapter that all organisations have a formal and informal communication system, and that communication flows horizontally, vertically and diagonally through the organisation. At least it should flow; sometimes it gets blocked, sometimes it gets distorted, sometimes it gets lost. When these problems arise, it can be potentially damaging for your learners, because you may pass on incorrect information or not be aware of information that they need. Telling learners the wrong date for their examination, or omitting to tell them about an increase in registration fees (because nobody had told you!), can create resentment and frustration and certainly doesn't enhance their experience of learning. Let's look at some practical consequences of messages going astray and getting distorted.

Messages go astray

With the best will in the world, some messages don't reach the intended recipient in time, or at all, and sometimes they go to the wrong place. This case study illustrates a few of the things that can go wrong.

> ### CASE STUDY
> **Nobody ever tells you anything in this place!**
> Bashir is not a happy man. He is a part-time lecturer in computer studies and is in the middle of a DTLLS course. Here is an extract from his reflective journal:
>
> *Yesterday was a rotten day. I want to do the best for my students, but I seem to be constantly being messed about, never seem to be told anything in time and often it's wrong anyway. Yesterday was a good example. Just before I was due to teach my 11.00 BTEC National group Jenny, the secretary, said that I mustn't forget the 12.15 staff meeting. Well firstly, I hadn't been told about the meeting anyway, and secondly, I wouldn't finish my class till 12.30 and I'd already promised Jonathan, who is struggling with his PowerPoint presentation, that I would give him a hand after the class. So, either I had to cut the class short and cancel Jonathan's tutorial or be late for the meeting. Jenny said that her assistant had promised to tell me about the meeting, but Peter, our curriculum leader, wanted everyone to be there because he needed to sort out next year's programme.*
>
> *So I did cut the class short, and they weren't too chuffed because their next assignment is due in on Thursday and lots of them wanted help. The best I could offer was an extra half hour at 12.30 next Tuesday. Then, to cap it all, when I got back to the conference room, I found the meeting had been postponed because Peter had had to stand in for the Principal who was off sick! I then became pretty cross with Jenny, because when I asked her why she hadn't told me about the postponement, she said I'd just started teaching and she didn't want to interrupt. And guess when the meeting has been postponed to – next Tuesday at 12.30!*

PRACTICAL TASK PRACTICAL TASK **PRACTICAL TASK** PRACTICAL TASK **PRACTICAL TASK**

What has gone wrong with the communication between the people in this case study? Note ways in which the problems could have been avoided or overcome. And what should Bashir do about his 12.30 class next Tuesday? Compare your responses with the comments below.

You might think that all the characters in this study could have communicated more effectively. Peter seemed happy to arrange a meeting that interfered with normal class times, and certainly didn't check to see that everyone could come. Jenny doesn't seem to have advertised the meeting in writing (e-mail, memo or notice board), but instead relied on word of mouth. She hadn't asked for confirmation of who could come and who couldn't. She could also have found some way to get a message to Bashir while he was teaching, because of the urgency of the situation; perhaps a note handed to him to minimise interruption. It also looks as though Jenny's assistant didn't pass the message on. So the learning points here are to make sure that important messages are written and that recipients acknowledge receipt.

As for Bashir, he's been put in a difficult situation because he didn't receive the message on time. But this has happened and he has to deal with it. My view is that as his class has suffered a fair bit already, he should make strong representation to his curriculum leader to attend the meeting after his tutorial, and pick up points he has missed later. This could perhaps be done by e-mail or memo, or by a face-to-face chat, or both. Either way, if he does nothing, there is a good chance that such problems will recur, as Peter, Jenny and her assistant will not be made aware of the consequences of their sloppy communication habits.

There is a general point that arises from Bashir's experience. As a part-time lecturer he could feel left out of the communication network because he is only at work for a limited time. But there are things that he can do to minimise the feeling of being isolated. Race and Pickford (2007, pp157–8) give a list of points that are relevant to his situation and which you might find useful:

- Talking to other part-timers and learning from their experience.
- Letting colleagues know where and how they can leave messages for you.
- Letting colleagues know when you will be out of contact and when you will be in next.
- Getting yourself copied into e-mail lists.
- Going to relevant meetings and catching up on meetings you can't attend.

Come to think of it, these are not bad tactics for full-time staff as well.

Messages get distorted

The apocryphal World War I story of the message that originally read *Send reinforcements, we're going to advance!* but became, *Send three and fourpence we're going to a dance!* after it was passed down the line, has its echoes in everyday life in all organisations, and colleges and training centres are no exception. Generally speaking, the longer the line of authority and the more people who receive and pass on any given message, the greater the chance of a lot of confusion for the end user.

This point can be illustrated with a story related by Marion, an external verifier (EV) for City & Guilds health and social care courses.

I remember when I first started as an EV, I was allocated to verify a diploma course at a college near Birmingham. So I wrote a letter to the college introducing myself, and suggesting that maybe I could visit in a few weeks to meet the course leader and have a look at some of the group's first assignments. Out of courtesy, I addressed this letter to the head of department, and sat back to await a reply. Nothing happened for about ten days, and I was just thinking of ringing the college when three enormous parcels arrived on my desk, which must have cost an arm and a leg in postage, and which turned out to be all the first assignments from the whole group, together with an apologetic note from the lecturer, from which it was quite evident she had burnt the midnight oil to get the scripts marked. And I'd only wanted to have a look at three or four scripts when I visited the college!

It later transpired that the head of department had told the section head about my letter, who had in turn told the course team leader, who had in turn told Anne, the poor lecturer responsible for the unit. By the time my message reached her, the original tentative suggestion that I might look at a few examples of learners' work during a future visit, had become a demand for all the first assignments to be marked and sent to me prior to my coming to the college.

So I learnt a few things from this little episode. Firstly, I now always contact the person who is running the course for which I am the EV, preferably by phone. Secondly, I always confirm with an e-mail what we have agreed. I will copy in whoever in the management chain needs to know, but I will never again trust one of my messages to be passed down accurately to the person who is actually doing the work, without checking that it has reached its destination intact.

REFLECTIVE TASK

Consider whether there was anything Anne, the final recipient of Marion's message, could reasonably have done to avoid the unnecessary extra work she undertook in advance of Marion's visit.

You may have thought of the following:

- contact Marion by phone or e-mail to confirm details of what was required;
- ask her course team leader for confirmation;
- ask her section head and/or head of department for a copy of Marion's letter.

In any event, the learning point is that it is always wise to confirm and clarify what is required, particularly when the request involves a lot of hard work.

Interpersonal communication with colleagues

We don't normally have the luxury of choosing the people we work with. On appointment, we come into an organisation where our colleagues are already there; we are the novices, they are the established community. Over time, we will establish close personal rapport with some of our colleagues, but there may well be some who we find difficult to get on with. It is relatively easy to communicate with the people we like, but it is much more likely that problems will arise in our communication with people who are apathetic or sometimes antagonistic towards us. This section suggests some strategies for coping with these situations, in both informal and formal communication settings

Informal communication: communicating with colleagues

The first stage in this communication strategy was covered in the previous chapter. Do you remember Alistair, the site supervisor who resented people who seemed to look down on him and who didn't value the contribution he made to the organisation? This case study illustrated the importance of being sensitive to other people who work with you and showing through your communication that you value and respect them and the job they are doing. If you do, the chances are that their communication with you will reciprocate this sensitivity and respect and you will be able to work well together, to the benefit of both you and your learners.

Sometimes this doesn't happen, and you can still be on the receiving end of apathy and antagonism. The statement over the phone, *I'll call you back later!* or *I'll get the marked assignments back to you by Tuesday at the latest!* can mean that the speaker won't do anything at all. This leads us on to a second stage of an effective communication strategy in dealing with colleagues, and to explain this we need to consider the concept of roles and professionalism in a bit more detail.

In enacting their work roles, others in your role set will expect you to behave in a professional way, and this is a mutual feeling. An important strand of this is a high standard of professional ethics, behaviour and work activities while doing your job. Your colleagues will expect you, for example, to turn up to classes on time, respect confidentiality, mark work objectively and promptly, and not show undue favour for learners or colleagues that you particularly like. In return, you will expect the same professional standard from them. This professional behaviour is, to a large extent, expressed in communication, such as in the memos and e-mails that you send, and in the way you speak to and interact with other people.

In some ways this makes communication with someone you don't like much easier. Beyond showing respect and sensitivity for others, the expectation is that a professional approach involves maintaining the same standards of communication no matter who you are communicating with. This means being clear, dispassionate and objective. If you receive a message that is aggressive, this is no reason to reply in kind. It takes two to conduct a slanging match in a corridor; best make sure you are not the second person in this situation.

CASE STUDY

Jason and Gita

Jason is a newly appointed tutor in Life and Social Skills, and is currently teaching a small and quite demanding group of learners on an Entry level BTEC Certificate in Life Skills. He is planning to get all his learners to role-play a job interview in next Thursday's class.

However, there is a problem. His normal teaching room is far too small and cramped for the pairs exercise that he wants to conduct in the role play, with six pairs of learners interviewing each other simultaneously. An ideal solution would be to swap rooms with Gita, a part-time tutor, who teaches a numeracy class at the same time, just across the corridor. The advantage here is that her room is much larger and has little alcoves where it should be possible to set up the interviews with a bit of privacy. The disadvantage is that Gita has been singularly un-cooperative recently, and Jason suspects that this might be because she applied for Jason's job and resents his appointment.

While Jason is mulling over how to approach Gita, an e-mail arrives. This is it.

To: Jason Fletcher
From: Gita Hussein
Subject: Complaint about your BTEC CLS class

I am getting completely fed up with tidying up after your CLS class. This morning I found the room with all the furniture re-arranged, and I had to spend 10 minutes putting it back before I could start my class. It's been the same since the start of term, and I think you are being quite thoughtless about people using the room for the next session.

If you think that having a full-time job entitles you not to care about whoever uses your room after you, then you are very much mistaken. If this happens again, I will make a formal complaint to Susan.*

Gita H

(*Susan Howard, Jason's line manager)

Jason's immediate reaction to reading this was one of anger. *How dare she threaten me in this way! I've never moved the furniture around. It has always been set out like this when I have arrived to take my class and I've always left it just as I found it. Anyway, why didn't she ask me about it before if it has been such a problem? And why not just have a quiet word rather than rushing into print? And that remark about having a full-time job is really out of order. I've a good mind to take it round to Susan now and get my own complaint in first!* Jason's second reaction was to think a bit more before he did anything. After all, he did want Gita's goodwill for next week's room swap, and the class would be very disappointed if the interviews had to be either cancelled or held in the normal room.

PRACTICAL TASK PRACTICAL TASK **PRACTICAL TASK** PRACTICAL TASK **PRACTICAL TASK**

1. Comment on Gita's way of communicating with Jason. Did she demonstrate a professional approach to a colleague? How could her approach be improved?
2. How should Jason respond to Gita's e-mail in order to resolve the issue of furniture arrangement?
3. How and when should Jason raise the issue of swapping rooms with Gita so his class can enact its interview role play in an appropriate environment?

Compare your responses with the comments below.

One of the things to consider is what Gita was trying to achieve by writing this message. If we take it at face value, she wants Jason to arrange the room in a way she thinks is normal, although it isn't clear what this is. She would probably have achieved this by talking to Jason and explaining what she wanted. This would also have allowed Jason to explain what he had done, and there is the basis for an agreement on how Jason should leave the room in future. The tone of the e-mail is aggressive and personalised and is almost calculated to cause offence; a case of letting one's feelings override the professional role of negotiating with a colleague. Elephant behaviour is clearly on display here.

Jason is in the tricky position of wanting a favour from a colleague who has shown personal resentment towards him. The fact that her complaint is based on the false premise that Jason had moved the furniture himself does, however, give him a little leverage. As in Gita's case, this may best be resolved by a chat rather than a reply by e-mail. This would give

Jason the opportunity to explain the background, and to negotiate what to do with the furniture in future so that both are happy. Similarly, he could raise the issue of the room swap if and when he felt he had established a reasonable dialogue with Gita.

One final comment; Jason has a good case for complaint about Gita's comments on his appointment. I do not think they should be ignored. Being sensitive to other people's feelings does not mean that unprofessional behaviour should be condoned. The important thing is to raise the issue in a non-confrontational way, to respond objectively and avoid personal rancour. And there is always recourse, as a last resort, to take any matter higher up the management chain if it cannot be solved amicably between the people directly involved.

Formal communication: one-to-one discussions and interviews

There is a range of face-to-face formal communication settings that you are likely to encounter in your role as a teacher. They are formal in the sense that they are recorded in greater or lesser detail, sometimes just the outcomes, sometimes including a narrative of the discussion. These occasions will include interviews, formal meetings with a line manager, applications for staff development courses, appraisals, review meetings with verifiers and so on.

The principles that we have discussed in previous chapters are just as relevant here as in communicating with learners, and this can be illustrated by continuing the story of Jason and Gita.

CASE STUDY
Jason and Gita continued (along with Susan)
While Jason was still mulling over what to do about Gita's e-mail, Susan Howard (Jason's line manager) popped her head round the door and said, *I gather there's a problem with Gita. Let's talk about it at this afternoon's meeting.* Then she was gone, but the grapevine was obviously still alive and flourishing.

The meeting Susan referred to is a regular monthly meeting between Jason, as a newly appointed tutor, and his line manager. This is a part of the college's quality programme, whereby all newly appointed staff have a regular monthly meeting to review progress and discuss any problems. Outcomes are recorded and agreed by both parties before being placed on staff personal files and reviewed at the end of the first year of employment.

PRACTICAL TASK PRACTICAL TASK **PRACTICAL TASK** PRACTICAL TASK **PRACTICAL TASK**

What points about the problem with Gita do you think Jason should raise at the meeting with Susan? Should he say anything about his plan to swap rooms with Gita next week? What do you feel would be the best outcome for Jason from this meeting? Should he contact Gita? If so, when, how and for what purpose?

Note your responses and compare them to the comments below.

Susan clearly knows about Gita's feelings, and it is important that Jason explains the background to the furniture problem dispassionately and in a non-confrontational manner. I think the issue of a room swap is probably best dealt with directly with Gita in the first instance, to avoid any impression of going over her head. If there is time, a quick phone call or e-mail to Gita to suggest a chat to resolve the problem may well be a good idea. This would enable Jason to tell Susan that he is trying to do this directly with Gita rather than dragging Susan in as some sort of arbitrator.

From this, we can define some general guidelines about effective communication strategy that are particularly relevant to formal face-to-face meetings.

- Be clear about the purpose of the meeting. If, for example, your course is being reviewed, you need to know what aspects are being covered, and what outcomes are possible.
- Know what you want to get out of the meeting. If you are having a discussion about your own staff development, you need to be clear about what staff development activities you wish to be involved with in the coming year.
- Anticipate what your colleague is likely to raise at the meeting, and prepare an appropriate response. If the meeting is with your line manager who has previously commented on large photocopying costs, have your answer ready.
- Do not raise topics that are not within the scope of the meeting, but leave them to a more appropriate occasion. For example, a request for more textbooks should not be raised in a meeting to discuss difficulties experienced by a learner with dyslexia.
- Respect confidentiality. If a learner has told you in confidence about difficulties at home, this should not be revealed in a course review meeting without their permission.
- Avoid personal comments about other colleagues, such as those made by Gita in the previous case study.

All this can be summarised under the heading of adopting a professional approach; prepare well, know what you want, and be clear and objective.

Group communication

Your professional role as a teacher involves being a member of a group, in fact of many groups. Apart from the obvious role as a member of your college or training organisation, you will belong to a variety of groups: faculty, department, course team, examination board, curriculum specialist team, to name but a few of the possibilities. To function, all these groups must have a communication system, and this is invariably through the medium of meetings. Meetings play such an important part in an organisation's operations that it is no surprise that one of the most popular videos produced by Video Arts, a leading provider of training videos, is entitled *Meetings Bloody Meetings!*, which was followed up by an equally popular one called *More Bloody Meetings!* These titles encapsulate the love–hate relationship that most teachers have towards meetings: on the one hand they are tedious and time-consuming, on the other they seem to be the only way of getting things done.

So you will certainly be a member of several groups at work, and the consequence is that you will attend lots of meetings. Many of these meetings will directly affect your learners; course review meetings and exam boards are obvious examples. If you can communicate effectively in this arena, you will be enhancing their learning experience. First, however, we need to look at the characteristics of groups in contrast to interpersonal communication, before looking at how these features apply to meetings.

Features of groups

All the principles of effective interpersonal communication are applicable to group communication. Group membership, however, implies additional processes that are not likely to occur in discussions between two people. First, the group has an identity of its own. Burton and Dimbleby describe how:

> when we are part of a group the dynamics of the group, its tasks and social relationships mean that we are more conscious of playing a role and of being concerned with the group. The group, when it's working cohesively, develops a life of its own of which the individual members are merely a part – we subordinate our individual needs and motives for the sake of the group.
>
> (Burton and Dimbleby, 1988, p178)

A second feature of group communication is that members adopt specific roles in relating to the other members of the group. Some members may be naturally quiet, and take a passive role in group meetings, in contrast to more extravert members who contribute a lot. Meredith Belbin (1993) identified nine different roles in group transactions, which have since been updated and are summarised below.

Role name	Strengths and styles
Coordinator:	able to get others to work together; confident, clear thinker;
Shaper:	motivated, energetic, assertive, competitive, prone to impatience;
Plant:	innovative, often radical, creative, original, imaginative, unorthodox, problem-solving, not interested in detail;
Monitor–Evaluator:	serious, prudent, critical thinker, analytical, conservative, not a motivator;
Implementer:	systematic, common sense, loyal, structured, reliable, practical, efficient, unimaginative;
Resource Investigator:	networker, outgoing, affable, negotiator, can lose interest after initial stages;
Team Worker:	supportive, adaptable, perceptive, listener, mediator, can be indecisive;
Completer–Finisher:	attention to detail, accurate, high standards, gets task done on schedule, worrier;
Specialist:	technical expert, perfectionist in specialist area, does not have overall vision.

Belbin's main point was that the more diverse the group, the better the chance of it being successful, and that an effective team consists of those with different strengths and styles.

REFLECTIVE TASK

Which of Belbin's categories do you feel is most appropriate to you? How is this reflected in your communicative behaviour in work groups?

A third feature of communication in groups is that it tends to reflect group norms, the accepted standards of behaviour that the group has developed. Sometimes a tendency towards conformity arises, known as *groupthink.* This characteristic arises in mature groups that are cohesive to the extent that the task becomes secondary to avoiding conflict and maintaining group unity. So there are dangers in too much agreement as well as in too little. Ellis and McClintock describe this phenomenon.

> *In a group, which perceives itself as cohesive, effective and a successful unit, communication will be aimed towards minimising conflict and maintaining cohesion. Since non-conformity might damage the cohesion, members who privately disagree with the views expressed by the leader, and supported by the majority, may be unwilling to risk conflict by publicly admitting that they disagree.*
>
> (Ellis and McClintock, 1994, p117)

REFLECTIVE TASK

Have you ever attended a meeting where you have experienced the groupthink phenomenon? Consider whether this has affected the outcomes of the meeting.

Meetings

One of the prerequisites of effective communication and behaviour in meetings is a clear understanding of the purpose of the meeting and why you are there. Different types of meetings require different responses from those attending. Here are some of the most common forms of meetings that you are likely to encounter.

- Briefings: mainly used for dissemination of information on particular topics. Departmental meetings where members of staff are brought up to date with events and policy changes are examples of this type of meeting.
- Reviews: course committee meetings to evaluate specific courses and reviews of learner progress.
- Planning meetings: meetings to decide future events, such as the introduction of new courses.
- Negotiations: meetings to resolve specific conflicts, such as division of resources between competing bidders.
- Brainstorming: meetings to gather new ideas such as a meeting to consider how to market a new series of courses.
- Quality circles and working parties: meetings to consider operational issues which are causing problems or need to be improved, such as a meeting to resolve car parking problems at an overcrowded site.

This list is not exhaustive, and you may well find yourself involved in other types of meetings. But your role will vary depending on the type and purpose of the meeting.

PRACTICAL TASK PRACTICAL TASK **PRACTICAL TASK** PRACTICAL TASK **PRACTICAL TASK**

List the meetings you are required to attend in your present job. For each meeting state the following:
- type of meeting;
- purpose of meeting;
- your role in the meeting.

Compare your responses with your colleagues and with the comments below.

Your response to this task should help you clarify the types of meetings you most commonly attend and what their main purposes are. It also brings us back to the idea of role and how this is enacted in your particular situation. For example, if you attend a lot of briefings, the chances are that your role will be that of listener, and of asking questions to confirm what actions you may have to take. By contrast, if you attend brainstorming sessions, the expectation is that your contribution will be much more positive, offering ideas, comparing approaches and encouraging colleagues to do the same. A review meeting requires you to provide information on your particular area of expertise or about your own learners, consequently involving careful preparation.

In summary, in order to behave and communicate effectively in meetings, there are some guidelines to follow.

- Know the type of meeting you are being asked to attend and what its purpose is.
- Know why you are invited and what you are expected to do; in other words, be clear about your role.
- Know the rules of the game. In a formal meeting this includes the rules of procedure, and in all meetings this includes unspoken conventions, such as how decisions are reached and recorded.
- Do your homework prior to the meeting. Read the relevant documents and work out what you will need to say on particular agenda items.
- Play yourself in by listening to and observing other members in action. You will soon realise what sort of contribution is likely to be accepted and what sort rebuffed.

Leading groups

Not only are you likely to spend a lot of time attending meetings, but you will also probably find yourself having to organise and manage some groups. For example, as a course leader you may well be responsible for meetings of the course team, or you may be asked to lead a group on a particular task such as organising a display. This leads us to a consideration of leadership and, in particular, how a group leader communicates effectively with group members and manages group communication.

Libraries have shelves of books on effective leadership, most of them outside the scope of this book. One school of thought, however, is relevant to the close relationship of effective communication and effective leadership. Kurt Lewin, writing in the 1940s, theorised that good leadership was a matter of communication style, and the thesis is well summarised by Burton and Dimbleby.

> *A leader requires considerable communication skill in order to manage other people and in order to achieve group goals. Theoretically, a person who has effective communication and social skills – ability to express and to read verbal and non-verbal messages, to perceive other people's needs and to maintain open social relationships – is likely to be an effective leader.*
>
> (Burton and Dimbleby, 1988, p172)

Lewin (1948) identified three distinct styles of leadership. First, authoritarian leadership relies on personal authority and power to make decisions and assigns others to carry them out. The dominant communication is the issuing of directives. This style can have the advantage of getting things done promptly, but has the disadvantage that members of the group feel disempowered and reluctant to contribute and use their own initiative. Second, by contrast, democratic-style leaders encourage contributions from others who share in the decision-making process. Communication is predominantly discussion and consultation. The main advantage is that all members feel valued and part of the decision-making process; the disadvantage is that meetings tend to be long and decision making slow. Finally, a *laissez-faire* leadership style indicates a passive role, in which the leader does not use their power to lead but merely lets the group proceed as it wishes. Communication here will, at best, be constructive discussion, at worst, aimless conversation. It is difficult to see any advantage in this leadership style.

REFLECTIVE TASK

What is your preferred leadership style? Consider how this is reflected in the communication patterns you have observed in recent meetings.

The way you communicate as a group leader will be a reflection of your leadership style. However, this does not mean that you cannot adapt when the occasion demands it. If you tend to the autocratic style, you may recognise when it is important to allow discussion for the sake of group morale. If your preferred style is democratic, there may be occasions when you have to be more direct and limit discussion in order to meet an important deadline. The following case study illustrates how some of this adaptability is important in managing a small team of colleagues.

CASE STUDY
Gavin's sports course

Gavin has been team leader for a City & Guilds level 2 course in Sports Operations for six months. Next week, the EV is visiting to review course work and Gavin is worried about the course team meeting he has arranged to prepare for this visit, so he is seeking advice from his colleague and friend David, who works in Construction Crafts and is a team leader himself.

The problem is that the last meeting we had was a disaster, and I can't afford the same sort of shambles with the EV coming next Tuesday. We were trying to review problems with individual students. Firstly, nobody remembered that we were planning to discuss the progress of students who had given us problems, and so they were just speaking from memory. Then Heather was half an hour late, and I had to waste ten minutes telling her what we'd discussed. Even then, she didn't contribute anything useful; just complained about next year's enrolment, which wasn't even relevant to the meeting. On the other hand, I couldn't stop Russell talking. He went on and on about one of his students with dyslexia needing special support, and everyone else was getting impatient because they wanted to talk about their students' problems and Russell was hogging the discussion. The end result was that we didn't get through the agenda and I know people left feeling that it was a waste of time. Jonathan, who hadn't said anything during the meeting, saw me afterwards and said it would have been better if I'd just told everyone what to do and left it at that.

The thing is that I want everyone to have their say at these meetings, but we never seem to have time to do that and we all feel frustrated at the end. Well, it can't happen this time; all the coursework has to be handed in and marked before the EV comes, and we have to agree on what issues we wish to raise with her. So what do you think I should do to get to that stage without upsetting the team?

PRACTICAL TASK PRACTICAL TASK **PRACTICAL TASK** PRACTICAL TASK **PRACTICAL TASK**

Can you suggest any actions that Gavin should have taken to avoid or minimise the problems he encountered at the previous team meeting? In the light of this, what communication strategy should he employ prior to, and during, the forthcoming meeting? Note your responses and compare with the comments below.

I think David could give some pointers to Gavin about his communication with the group. They might include the following.

- Gavin could send a memo or e-mail to all members prior to a meeting. In the case of the forthcoming meeting, this would include telling them what the agenda is, what they should do with their coursework, and prepare the issues they want to discuss with the EV.
- He needs to be assertive enough to tell people when they are getting off the point. In this instance, it means being prepared to confront Heather if she introduces irrelevant topics.
- He could have a word with Heather about the need to arrive on time or at least let him know in advance if this is a problem.
- He could agree with the group about limiting discussion on particular learners so everyone gets a chance to contribute. This might well avoid the situation that arose with Russell.
- He needs to ensure that everyone is invited to speak, thus avoiding Jonathan's resentment at others dominating the meeting.

A SUMMARY OF **KEY POINTS**

> In any organisation, messages will get blocked, distorted and lost. Effective communication strategies can minimise the consequences.

> Showing respect and sensitivity for others is a good basis for effective interpersonal communication with colleagues.

> A professional approach to communicating with colleagues requires a dispassionate and objective communication style.

> Interpersonal communication in formal settings requires you to prepare well, know what you want and be clear and objective.

> Communication in groups is influenced by the identity, maturity and composition of the group.

> Effective communication in meetings requires thorough preparation and an understanding of type, purpose and nature of the meeting.

> Effective management of meetings requires an adaptive and flexible leadership style.

Branching options

The following tasks are designed to help you consolidate and develop your ability to communicate effectively with colleagues.

Reflection

Consider the preparation you need to undertake for a formal appraisal interview. Would your relationship to your appraiser influence the way you communicated during the interview? If so, in what way?

Analysis

Select one of your work groups or teams. Identify which of the Belbin categories your colleagues predominantly belong to, and how this is reflected in their communication style.

Research

Investigate recent research into leadership styles. To what extent are your findings applicable to organisations in the lifelong learning sector in general and to your organisation in particular?

REFERENCES AND FURTHER READING

Belbin, M (1993) *Team roles at work*. Oxford: Butterworth-Heinemann.

Burton, G and Dimbleby, R (1988) *Between Ourselves: An introduction to interpersonal communication*. London: Edward Arnold.

Evans, D (2000) *People, communication and organisations*. Harlow: Longman.

Ellis, R and McClintock, A (1994) *If you take my meaning: theory into practice in human communication*. London: Edward Arnold.

Hartley, P (1999) *Interpersonal communication*. London: Routledge.

Lewin, K (1948) *Resolving social conflicts*. London: Harper and Row.

LLUK (2006) *New overarching professional standards for teachers, tutors and trainers in the lifelong learning sector*. London: LLUK.

Ludlow, R and Panton, F (1992) *The essence of effective communication*. Hemel Hempstead: Prentice Hall.

Race, P and Pickford, R (2007) *Making teaching work*. London: Sage Publications.

11
Resources

This chapter will help you to:

- understand the principles that underpin the selection and use of teaching resources;
- identify and select appropriate resources that support your communication with learners;
- recognise the effects of ILT in resource provision;
- incorporate ILT into your teaching resources.

Links to LLUK professional standards for QTLS:

AS3, AS4, AS7, AK4.2, AP4.2, AK5.1, AK5.2, AP5.1, AP5.2, AK7.1, AP7.1, BS2, BS3, BS5, BK1.3, BP1.3, BK2.2, BK2.3, BP2.2, BP2.3, BK3.1, BK3.3, BK3.4, BK3.5, BP3.1, BP3.3, BP3.4, BP3.5, BK5.1, BK5.2, BP5.1, BP5.2, DK1.2, DP1.2, FK1.2, FP1.2.

Links to CTLLS:

Unit 1 Preparing to teach in the lifelong learning sector;

Unit 2 Planning and enabling learning.

Links to DTLLS:

Unit 1 Preparing to teach in the lifelong learning sector;

Unit 2 Planning and enabling learning;

Unit 4 Theories and principles for planning and enabling learning;

Unit 5 Continuing personal and professional development;

Unit 7 Wider professional practice.

Introduction

The emphasis of this book has been on teachers and their personal ability to communicate effectively. Sometimes, actually nearly always, teachers need help, and this help is available in the form of teaching resources. There are now more and better resources that we can access than ever before. However, the choice and complexity of this vast range is daunting, and this chapter is written to help you to choose and make best use of the resources that you have access to.

It used to be relatively simple to review the range of resources that we could use. There were materials for giving information to learners, such things as handouts and task sheets. Then there were display aids, like whiteboards, posters, flip charts and OHPs. But then, along came computers, and suddenly teachers were plunged into a world of technology, with a language of its own and a frightening array of electronic wizardry that the learners were often more skilled at mastering than the teachers. We are still living in this new world, and the only certainty seems to be that the pace of change will continue and accelerate.

However, some things do remain the same. The qualities of good teaching resources apply just as much to interactive whiteboards as they do to flip charts. So the first part of this chapter concentrates on the principles that underpin effective resource use, and gives a brief review of the teaching resources most commonly in use in the lifelong learning sector. The second part of the chapter looks at change, particularly how technological developments have affected and enhanced the role of the teacher and how this is likely to develop in the near future.

There is one thing to emphasise about the content of this chapter: it is concerned primarily with teaching resources (i.e. resources that a teacher will use to communicate with learners) because this book is focused on teachers' communication skills. The distinction between these resources and learning resources (i.e. resources that are primarily used by learners) is somewhat arbitrary. Some resources, a gapped handout for example, fall into both categories. If you need more detailed coverage of the whole range of resources, the topic is well covered in recent books on teacher training such as Reece and Walker (2007), Scales (2008) and Petty (2009).

Choosing and using teaching resources

There are several principles that apply to choosing and using resources effectively in a teaching environment.

Use the learners' dominant sense: sight

By far the most common reason to use resources other than your voice is that this gives the opportunity to supplement your learners' sense of hearing, most particularly by using their sense of sight. The latter is by far the strongest sense, probably accounting for about 75% of what we learn, as distinct from about 12% of what we hear. If you don't make use of it, something else most certainly will. It may be the interesting view outside the classroom window or your habit of pacing backwards and forwards across the room. In any event, these visual stimuli will distract learners from your message if you rely entirely on speech to transmit it. Using visual aids such as boards, PowerPoint presentations and flip charts to reinforce your message effectively fulfils several purposes.

- You get learners' attention, and reduce the chances of their being distracted by other things or people (perhaps including some of your own mannerisms).
- You add variety to your lessons and arouse interest.
- You help your learners understand concepts. A cake (or a drawing of one) divided into six slices gives learners a better understanding of fractions than an explanation of what *one-sixth* means.
- You reinforce learning and aid retention by repetition and by supplementing your voice with visual stimuli.

Use a variety of resources

However professional your resources look, even the most dedicated learner will lose interest if they are subjected to an endless procession of PowerPoint slides or are forever required to fill in gapped handouts. I don't know what the attention span of your learners is like, but for some of my classes it is extremely short and seems to be getting shorter with every year that passes. So in addition to varying learner activity, it's a good idea to vary your resources as well.

Design and adapt your resources to the needs and abilities of your audience

Your teaching resources need to be appropriate for your group of learners, and to start with you need to know their capabilities. Can they understand the language that your resources use? Have they sufficient ICT skills to access and manipulate the computer-based resources you wish to use? Do you allow sufficient time for your learners to assimilate the information you are presenting to them? Learners of different ages present different problems. On the one hand, teenagers can give you a lesson on texting, but may have difficulty in communicating face-to-face. On the other, older learners may have a lot of difficulty with e-mail and be terrified of ICT. More of this later in the chapter.

You also need to know the capabilities of individuals, particularly in the case of learners who suffer from a disability. A partially sighted learner, for example, may need handouts in large print, and may need to be positioned close to any board display to ensure they can see it clearly.

Ensure your resources are produced to a high professional standard

As we saw in Chapter 4, the resources that you use, particularly written material given to learners, reflect your own standards of presentation. One of the real advantages of computer technology is that it gives all of us the capability to produce materials to a standard that previously could only be attained by commercial printers. This puts you in a strong position to demand similar standards from your learners.

Design your resources to maximise impact

Pictures send stronger messages than words, as any newspaper editor will tell you, and colour sends a stronger signal than greyscale. If your aim is to arouse interest and grab your learners' attention, use colour, diagrams and pictures.

Ensure you are competent to manage your resources

Some sophisticated resources, such as an interactive whiteboard linked to a computer, clearly need some familiarisation and practice before you can be confident of using them effectively. But even simpler skills, such as writing on a chalkboard, are not as easy as they look. So make sure you review, prepare and practise using your resources before you face a group of learners. This is particularly true concerning the use of ICT equipment, as many younger learners may well be far more expert on this type of equipment than you are.

Remember, resources are there to help, not replace, you

The important word in the phrase *audio visual aids* is the word *aids*. It is a reminder that teaching resources are there to support you in your role as a facilitator of learning and not to take your place. There is an attraction and temptation in much new technology to overuse it because it is so versatile and produces such excellent results. This is particularly evident in PowerPoint presentations where, at the extreme, you can become little more than a computer operator, impressing your audience with an array of sound and visual effects that provides a distraction from the learning points rather than a reinforcement of them. This tendency to overuse technology can also encourage you to be a *sage on the stage*, providing lots of visual tricks but not really guaranteeing that your learners actually learn anything. Remember the basic tenet that learners learn more effectively by being actively involved.

REFLECTIVE TASK

Think of the resources that you are using for one of your courses, and consider to what extent the way you have selected and used them is in accord with the principles outlined above.

Teaching resources: a brief overview

The first thing to remember is that the teaching resources available to you comprise more than a collection of audio visual aids. The environment you are operating in and the people that inhabit it are just as important a resource as the aids you use to reinforce your message. Let's look at each of these areas in turn.

The environment

The first thing to take into account is a resource that is often taken for granted: the teaching room and the furniture in it. You probably can't select the room, but you can usually do something about arranging the furniture in order to establish a good learning environment. This means, apart from the obvious requirements for space and comfort, that the learners should all be able to see and hear you and the resources that you are using. This is easier said than done in some situations. For example, in a room equipped with PCs, the monitors can obstruct the learners' view of a whiteboard, and it may be necessary to gather the learners in a group at the front of the room in order to use this display aid. Similarly, in a practical workshop situation, large benches fixed to the floor can inhibit a teacher's demonstration, and you may have to move learners around so that they can see what is going on.

Your resource environment may also include a Learning Resource Centre (LRC). Known in ancient times (such as when I started teaching) as libraries, LRCs are now commonly a central resource in educational organisations. LRCs house not only books and journals, but also banks of computers, DVDs, printing and photocopying facilities and much else. LRCs are much more likely to be used as a learning resource rather than a teaching resource but, nevertheless, can provide you with a rich source of material and facilities to make your resources comprehensive and professional. Therefore it's a good idea to get on good terms with the LRC manager and staff.

People

Some years ago the term *Personnel* went out of fashion in management studies and was replaced by *HR, Human Resources*. Although I've always thought *HR* was cumbersome, it does at least have the advantage of stressing that people are resources, and in a teaching context your most valuable resource can be your learners themselves. Their experience can be used to illustrate your learning points more powerfully than a whole range of handouts and slides. The interview experience of a learner who has just been successful in getting a job and is attending a Return to Work course or the child-minding experience of a learner on a Diploma in Child Care programme provide unique examples that can be drawn on to illustrate learning points. And don't forget to use your own experience to illustrate your points. Again, this is unique material that brings a subject to life. There is a limit to the use of anecdotes to illustrate points, but examples from real life are always likely to be remembered longer than theoretical examples.

Audio visual aids

There is potentially a very wide range of audio visual aids (AVAs) or just visual aids (VAs) available to you that will harness your learners' dominant sense of sight, and help you to transmit, explain and reinforce your message. I say potentially because you are clearly limited to the equipment that is available to you in your organisation. It's all very well waxing lyrical about PowerPoint presentations, but irrelevant if all you have in your class-room is a flipchart.

The range of AVAs that you are likely to come across is covered in detail in most textbooks on teacher education, such as Petty (2009) or Reece and Walker (2007), but they can be classified briefly as follows.

Presentation aids
These are aids that enable you to display your material for learners to see and possibly interact with. These aids include:

- boards of various types: whiteboards, chalkboards, magnetic boards, interactive whiteboards;
- flipcharts;
- overhead projectors (OHPs) and transparencies (OHTs);
- PowerPoint (includes computer, data projector and slides).

Commercially produced aids
These are aids where you effectively give some control over to the producer of the aid, and include:

- DVDs, films and film strips;
- wallcharts and displays;
- models and realia (the real thing).

Written material
Material that you give to learners to inform, assess or consolidate learning, including:

- handouts;
- worksheets;
- assignment briefs;
- photocopied material.

Assuming that you have a choice of AVAs available to you, let's have a look at how you would select the most suitable for your teaching purpose. I think there are two main criteria that AVAs should meet when considering which to use: suitability for the audience and practicality. Let's look at each of these in turn.

Suitability for the audience
We have already said that teaching resources need to take into account the needs and abilities of your audience. This is particularly true concerning AVAs. As we saw in Chapter 4, if you issue handouts that are written in a dense and opaque style to a group

of learners studying on a level 2 course, they are likely to find the content difficult to understand. So you need to tailor your resources to the previous knowledge and experience of your learners; a worksheet that uses jargon will only be understood if your learners have experience in the particular technical field that you are referring to.

Practicality

Practical considerations are also important in determining your selection of AVAs. One practical consideration is the time you have available. A 15-minute video clip can take a substantial bite out of a 45-minute lesson, and you need to make a judgement on whether it is actually worth your while to use it if the learning point could be made with a couple of PowerPoint slides. Also, a model that requires a lot of time to assemble and dismantle might not be so time-effective as a coloured wallchart.

Second, there is the nature of the aids themselves. Whereas some might be too large and cumbersome to move around easily, others may be too small for learners to see unless they are very close. These aids also need to be available and in working order. A PowerPoint presentation is useless without a serviceable projector, screen and possibly speakers: OHP transparencies are also useless if the projector bulb fails and there is no spare.

In summary, you should choose your resources on the basis of whether they are appropriate and practical for your purpose and for your learners.

PRACTICAL TASK PRACTICAL TASK **PRACTICAL TASK** PRACTICAL TASK **PRACTICAL TASK**

Identify the most suitable resources to teach a group of 20 motor vehicle learners how an alternator works from the following list:

- a real alternator;
- a model of an alternator which comes to pieces to show the constituent parts;
- handouts with a sectioned drawing of an alternator;
- a sectioned drawing of an alternator on a flip chart or whiteboard;
- a PowerPoint presentation of how an alternator works;
- a short commercial video of how an alternator works.

Compare your response with the comments below.

The answer to this task is, as always, *It depends* ... The things it depends on are such constraints as time, availability of projection equipment, quality of the commercial film and so forth. But a few general points can be made.

- The real alternator is probably not suitable, at least on its own, because it won't be possible for all the learners to see the detail, and it will be difficult to dismantle it so that the workings are clear for the learners to see.
- The model alternator is probably more fit for purpose because the components can be shown. There may, however, be problems in getting all 20 learners close enough to see the detail in the time allowed.
- The handouts are probably best suited for reinforcement, to be taken away after the class and used as an *aide-mémoire* by the learners.
- The board or flip chart drawing will take time to prepare, but at least avoid the disadvantage of possible equipment failure.
- The PowerPoint presentation is perhaps more effective than the board drawing because the teacher can

build up to a complete drawing starting from simple components, with the additional possibility of being able to add movement.

- The commercial video may be professionally slick and impressive, but remember you are to some extent handing the lesson over to the producer of the video.

Teaching resources and technology

If you were born in 1900, it would have seemed inconceivable that, within a lifetime, people would be able to travel anywhere in the world by air. Air travel was a fantasy in the minds of writers of science fiction. But for anyone born in 1950, air travel was a fact of life, and in addition, they could watch the world through television and talk to friends in Australia by phone, the stuff of dreams for their forebears. Nowadays, it is difficult to think of a world without computers and mobile phones, so we have a similar paradigm shift; the only difference is that it has occurred in less than half the time and shows no sign of slowing down.

The introduction of computers into education on a large scale over the past two decades has revolutionised the area of learning and teaching resources, as well as spawning a whole new language which seems to change every other year or so. First, we had information technology (IT), which is now used to refer to equipment such as PCs, scanners, printers, monitors and so on. This definition then developed into information and communication technology (ICT), referring to IT equipment connected to the internet or a local area network. Currently, the most commonly used terms are e-learning and information learning technology (ILT), denoting ICT specifically used to support teaching and learning. For simplicity, I will use ILT throughout this section.

There is a philosophical debate about the best way to use ILT, which is well summarised by Weller (2007), who defines two conflicting approaches. First, some see the internet as:

> an unprecedented delivery mechanism, because it can deliver content globally and at the user's demand ... [The other] viewpoint is the concept of the internet facilitating two-way communication... [that] encourages discussion, dialogue and community in a manner which is not limited by time or place. The role of educators in this world is to facilitate dialogue and support students.
>
> (Weller, 2007, p6)

My feeling is that we have become pretty good at using ILT as a content-focused delivery mechanism, but have some way to go to fulfil its potential as facilitating dialogue.

REFLECTIVE TASK

Which of these viewpoints do you agree with? As you read the rest of this section, consider whether the ideas discussed confirm or amend this viewpoint.

As teachers, we need to come to terms with ILT if we are to use resources effectively in communicating with our learners. This is easier said than done, because the pace of change has been so rapid that it is very difficult to keep up, and it's no wonder that sometimes we are struggling to communicate effectively in such a different world. The electronic revolution has dramatically affected our learners, our teaching environments and our organisations. This section looks at each of these aspects in turn.

ILT and people: learners and teachers

They have been called many things: generation Y, echo boomers and the Facebook generation to name but a few. These are the people, born since 1980, who have never known life without computers, the internet, mobile phones and video games, and cannot imagine life without them. Scales (2008) calls them digital natives. We often accuse some of our learners of living in another world. Well, actually, they do. It's called cyber space, and it has an existence and language all of its own. The language is called text, and the world is inhabited by blogs, chat rooms, MP3 players, Facebook, Twitter, iTunes and much else. For digital natives, life is impossible without a mobile phone, preferably the latest model, and it is a major disaster if it is lost.

By contrast, those who do remember life before the internet are digital immigrants; people, including me, who grew up without this technology, probably don't understand it and are somewhat frightened by it. Dorothy, who has just returned to education and is training to be a nurse, is a typical digital immigrant.

I don't really understand computers. My partner Peter has had a PC for the last few years, and I've just got round to getting a Hotmail account and sending e-mails to my friends. But Peter had to set it up for me, and I'm still frightened that if I press the wrong button something awful will happen. I've had a mobile phone for a while but it just tends to sit in the glove compartment of the car in case there is a breakdown. The last time I tried to use it to tell Peter I would be late home, the battery was flat, so I really must try to get used to it and use it more. And text is a real mystery. What is all this about predictive text anyway? I don't think I'd ever be able to get the hang of it, even though Clare my daughter has tried to teach me.

REFLECTIVE TASK

Are you a digital immigrant or a digital native? Consider the effect of this background on your communication with your learners.

So you might be faced with a whole class of digital natives who are far more expert with digital technology than you are, or conversely a group of learners who are scared witless by the thought of using computers. Or, of course, your class might be a mixture of the two groups. Consequently, we need to be aware of our learners' IT skills and to adapt our approach to take account of these skills, or lack of them. There is little point in sending material to learners by e-mail if some of your learners are afraid of communicating in this way.

We also need to consider our own attitude to using ILT. It is easy to say that we need to learn how to use the ILT equipment that's available to us, but putting this into practice is somewhat harder. Paul is aged 37 and has just been appointed to his first teaching post after 15 years in the catering industry.

The students are great, but I'm really anxious about using the IT equipment. For instance, all the classrooms have smart boards and all the other lecturers seem to be really expert at using them. The other week I sat in on a French class and the teacher was using the smart board with a BBC language programme with quizzes and interactive games. The learners were really into responding and very keen to contribute. It made me feel very inadequate.

I know I should know all about these boards, but honestly, I never seem to have the time to learn and practise. We had a briefing from the technician during induction, but I've forgotten half of what she said. So I just tend to use the boards as a screen to show PowerPoint presentations and collect the students' feedback on flip charts.

Here is a genuine digital immigrant talking, and there is substantial research evidence to confirm that Paul's fears are not uncommon. Armstrong et al (2005) noted that:

interactive whiteboards can actually reinforce teacher-centred styles of delivery . . . [and] when faced with a new technology a teacher is likely to make sense of it in terms of previous experience of older technologies. This suggests, for example, that many teachers are likely to use digital whiteboards as an extension of the non-digital whiteboard.

(Armstrong et al, 2005, p459)

These researchers concluded that there is more to effective use of ILT than just installing the hardware and the associated software. Without in-service support, training and time this expensive and sophisticated technology is likely to be underused. My point is that this support needs to take into account the fears and anxieties of a generation of digital immigrant teachers if we are to operate professionally in the ILT environment in which we are working.

ILT and the learning environment: the virtual classroom

Not only has ILT given us a range of sophisticated teaching aids located in traditional teaching rooms, but it has also made it possible to teach a group of learners irrespective of where they are. We saw in Chapter 8 that teachers whose learners may be at home or work need to communicate with them in a way that makes them feel understood, valued and supported. ILT can make it possible to do this, and this section gives a brief review of the currently available technology.

Communicating with learners at a distance has been popular for over 40 years, and the Open University has been a leader in this. But we have moved on from relying on course materials being sent through the post and telephone conversations between tutor and learner. ILT has provided us with much more effective communication, and the core of this technology is the development of virtual learning environments (VLEs) and access to the internet.

Virtual learning environments

VLEs are electronic systems designed specifically to support teachers and learners, and which can be used as a scaffold to support a distance learning programme or to supplement a traditional course.

VLEs are potentially a very powerful teaching resource, which can facilitate personalised, accessible and inclusive learning. Hill (2008) gives a comprehensive list of what VLEs can do, including the capacity to:

- *deliver course information;*
- *provide a course overview;*
- *structure and sequence learning;*
- *deliver learning activities;*
- *make resources available, including internet resources;*
- *communicate between learner and tutor;*
- *assess learners and provide feedback;*
- *monitor learner experience.*

(Hill, 2008, p69)

In summary, a VLE means that your learners can undertake a programme independent of set attendance times and locations. They can receive materials, have tutorials and be assessed online; hence the concept of the virtual classroom.

So how would this work in practice? Here is Tony, an engineering lecturer, talking about his experience of VLEs.

A couple of years ago the college decided to install a VLE and I was a bit doubtful about the whole thing, mainly because my own IT skills were a bit flaky. I could use PowerPoint pretty well as a presentation tool, and I was happy enough with e-mail but that was about my limit. I didn't use the VLE – it was called Moodle – until four of my learners, who were in the RAF, were posted to Cyprus for a couple of months, and wanted to keep up with the course. They had internet access out there, so I was able to send them my lesson notes, handouts and copies of the assignment they otherwise would have missed. In fact they completed it very quickly and I was able to mark it and send them feedback about a week before the rest of the class got their results.

Anyway, thus emboldened, I decided to set up a discussion forum with these four learners to post discussion topics and set up quizzes. They got really keen and the discussion was very rewarding. I think it only worked so well because the learners were so strongly moti-vated and I'm not sure how well it would have worked with some of the other, less keen, members of the class. But I'm happier and more confident about Moodle now and I'd like to see if I could use some of the other activity modules such as wikis and chat rooms.

I don't think any technology, however good, can match actually having the learners physi-cally there with you. The personal interaction and the social relationships that build up between learners during the course are so important. But if the college thinks of offering the course in a distance-learning mode, then the VLE will really come into its own.

PRACTICAL TASK PRACTICAL TASK **PRACTICAL TASK** PRACTICAL TASK **PRACTICAL TASK**

Tony mentioned that he could identify some advantages and limitations in using the VLE at his college. Do you agree and how could you use a VLE in your own teaching? And what does he mean by wikis and chat rooms? Note your responses and compare with the comments below.

My view is that VLEs offer an opportunity for you, as a teacher, to communicate and interact with your learners anywhere and at any time. A VLE will enable you to:

- communicate instantly with your learners via e-mail;
- send video and audio clips to your learners online, as well as course materials;

- communicate with your group of learners via bulletin boards which can be accessed at times to suit both you and your learners;
- set up discussions with your group of learners by use of discussion forums;
- arrange and conduct tutorials without regard to where either you, or your learners, are actually located;
- assess your learners, track their progress and discuss this with them promptly online;
- set up online group projects, which your learners can work on collaboratively.

Most of your digital native learners will know a lot about chat rooms, and probably contribute to several. In the context of VLEs a particular subject-based chat room will be a closed user group, and will allow for the group to have a real-time discussion online, probably moderated by the tutor.

A wiki is a collection of web documents. In a VLE, wikis can be used for group project work where the whole group can create and edit a document together, creating a collaborative project report.

The internet

Access to the internet is a gateway to seemingly unlimited resources to enhance your teaching. The problem is finding the particular nugget of information that you want. However, help is at hand if you are lost in the cyber jungle.

In addition to search engines like Google, there are a number of websites that are devoted to providing access to teaching and learning resources and are well worth the investment of some of your valuable time.

- The Excellence Gateway (http://excellence.qia.org.uk) is a massive website run by the Quality Improvement Agency (QIA), specifically for post-16 providers, and offering resources, support, advice and examples of good practice across the whole sector. It also provides access to other websites such as ACLearn and FERL that formerly provided independent support to the sector.
- Intute (www.intute.ac.uk) is another comprehensive site, run by a consortium of universities, which provides access to a wide range of subject-based resources classified into separate curriculum categories.
- Joint Information Systems Committee (www.jisc.ac.uk) concentrates on the development of ICT to support education and research. The Collections link on its website gives access to a wide range of relevant resources.
- The National Learning Network (NLN) has been superseded, but a great number of subject-specific materials are still available online via the NLN materials website (www.nln.ac.uk).

Have a look at these sites; they may save you a lot of time and work.

ILT and the organisation: the paperless college

Educational organisations have had to come to terms with ILT and the possibilities that it offers. A visit to any college today will reveal learning centres stacked with computers, plus classrooms similarly equipped and with data projectors and interactive whiteboards. But I think this is only the start, and this section takes a look at one particular development affecting teaching resources and communication systems that may be a pointer to how colleges will look in a few years' time. Welcome to the paperless college!

This concept is driven by two things. Firstly, there is the amount of paper generated by any college or training centre. It is enormous, difficult to store, difficult to access and increasing year by year. So why not get rid of it, and store all written material electronically? Secondly, if all of the college community, including teachers, administrators and learners, had access to this electronic store, then information could be accessed instantaneously, from anywhere in the world with an internet connection.

Many colleges in the UK are starting to go down this road. Some have done so by issuing course materials and handbooks electronically and dispensing with printed hard copies. A few organisations have gone much further; let's have a look at one.

CASE STUDY

The paperless college

Stephenson College in Leicestershire was a traditional vocational FE college until recently, when it embarked on a £15 million building programme on a new site, and the new building was designed with the idea of a paperless college in mind.

The goal was to have a college where all information is stored electronically, and this new college has been operational since 2005. Members of staff are issued with laptop computers and are able to access the electronic store either by wi-fi or by plugging in to any terminal either in college or, for that matter, anywhere in the world. Each full-time learner is issued with a memory stick that can be pre-loaded with the course information they require. All learners have immediate access to the college's LearnNet, which holds all course information and resources.

The college is organised into curriculum areas called clusters. Each cluster has staff areas, study areas for learners, classrooms and workshops. The staff areas are free from filing cabinets and desks designated for each member of staff; instead there are desks and access points to the e-store which teachers can use at will, together with small mail boxes for each staff member. Each teaching room is equipped with an interactive whiteboard, data projector and an access point to the electronic system. So a teacher at the start of a lesson completes the electronic register for the class, and downloads all the material they need for the particular lesson from their files in the electronic store.

So what is the effect of all this on a teacher who is used to a traditional paper-based organisation? Here is Susan talking about her job in the college.

One of the things I really like is not having to cart loads of files, handouts and lesson notes into each lesson. All I do is download whatever I want before the lesson starts from my teaching file. And the days of scrabbling through filing cabinets to locate some essential document which is in the wrong place are gone for ever. Also, paperless means less paper, not no paper, so I can still give my learners a hard copy of key handouts.

Actually, there have been some real advantages from the new-style staff areas. Apart from the absence of piles of documents littering desks and cabinets, the fact that no food or drink is allowed in these areas means that I take my break in the rest area at the end of the corridor, and meet colleagues from other curriculum areas that I'd never have met before.

I think that this links in to the philosophy behind the design, which is an ethos based on sharing. I have access through the e-store to all the academic information in the college, and the old idea that This is my stuff and it is kept in my locked cabinet, *certainly doesn't work here. It also means that we've cut down on duplication and, as a teaching team, we can use all the materials that each of us has contributed, as well as tapping in to similar materials used in the other clusters.*

There's one thing that has been essential in making the system work, and that is the technical back-up if things go wrong. Last weekend I had a problem accessing my files while I was working at home, but I contacted the network manager and it was fixed within the hour. So, for me, the system is working well but, without this sort of response, it could spell disaster.

REFLECTIVE TASK

Consider how your use of resources and communication with learners would be affected if you were working in a similar environment to Susan's. If there are advantages, is there any way they could be incorporated into your present job? You can find more detail on the Stephenson College project on the QIA website at www.excellencegateway.org.uk/page.aspx?o=192362.

A SUMMARY OF **KEY POINTS**

> To be effective, resources should be varied, have a high impact, be produced to a high standard and utilise learners' sense of sight.

> Your teaching environment and your learners can be effective resources, in addition to AVAs.

> You need to know the advantages and limitations of the resources that are available to you, and be competent in their use.

> AVAs should be practical and appropriate to the needs of your learners.

> ILT has provided the means to produce high-quality teaching resources, and to use them in communicating with learners irrespective of time and place.

> Our use of ILT needs to take account of the ILT skills and experience of learners, which can vary from very little to a level far in advance of our own.

> Current technological innovation in education, exemplified by the increased use of VLEs and the introduction of college-wide electronic storage systems, is likely to be the forerunner of greater and more rapid change in the future.

Branching options

The following tasks are designed to help you choose and use teaching resources effectively.

Reflection

Consider the ways in which you could make use of your learners' experience as an additional resource in your teaching. Try to incorporate this in one of your lessons and note the results.

Analysis

Choose a teaching aid which you use frequently, and ask a group of your learners what they regard as its advantages and limitations. Collate their responses and analyse any changes you might make in its design and use. Note your conclusions.

Research

Use the internet to research the concept of e-learning, and evaluate the extent to which e-learning may be incorporated into your professional life as a teacher in the future.

REFERENCES AND FURTHER READING REFERENCES AND FURTHER READING

Armitage, A et al (2003) *Teaching and training in post-compulsory education*. Buckingham: Open University Press.

Armstrong, V et al (2005) Collaborative research methodology for investigating teaching and learning: the use of interactive whiteboard technology. *Education Review*. 57:4, 457–69.

Hill, C (2008) *Teaching with e-learning in the lifelong learning sector*. Exeter: Learning Matters.

Minton, D (2005) *Teaching skills in further and adult education*. London: Thomson.

Petty, G (2009) *Teaching today*. Cheltenham: Nelson Thornes.

Reece, I and Walker, S (2007) *Teaching, training and learning*. Durham: Business Education Publishers.

Scales, P (2008) *Teaching in the Lifelong Learning Sector.* Buckingham: Open University Press.

Weller, M (2007) *Virtual learning environments*. Abingdon: Routledge.

Websites

www.excellencegateway.org.uk
www.intute.ac.uk
www.jisc.ac.uk
www.moodle.org
www.nln.ac.uk

Endpiece

This book started with a consideration of how we can all develop basic communication skills such as speaking, listening, reading and writing to become more effective teachers and to make the learning experience both enjoyable and exciting. Now we finish with a futuristic vision of a paperless educational world. This is quite a long journey, and en route it's easy to lose sight of the fundamentals of effective communication.

So the final thought is this. Regardless of all contemporary resources and technology, effective communication is essentially a simple concept. We pass messages to others, receive their messages and thus start a sophisticated process of thought and information transfer that is at the root of human development. Teaching and learning are central to this process, and both activities can be immensely frustrating and fulfilling in equal measure. To diminish the frustration and increase the fulfilment I think it's worth working hard at being better communicators; thus we inspire our learners and enjoy the intrinsic rewards of changing their lives. And then everyone benefits.

180424